Praise for *Celebr*

Spanning from the immediate post-war era through to the recent coronavirus pandemic, the stories and reflections held within this book are uplifting, amusing and thought-provoking. Written by two distinguished teacher-authors (and boasting a stirring foreword by Ben Bailey Smith), the book covers a range of settings, in which night schools, sports fields and breaktime clubs and more are considered alongside the regular classroom. *Celebrating Teachers* is simultaneously an insightful handbook and an inspirational guide for all teachers.

Dr James McGrath, Senior Lecturer in Literature and Creative Writing, Leeds Beckett University

In *Celebrating Teachers*, Gary and Chris share a wide range of poignant reminders of the impact we teachers can make – which often extend far beyond academic outcomes. It will be a useful resource for teachers in their early career and for the mentors who will support them.

Julie McBrearty, Principal, Welland Park Academy

Delivered in their trademark style, Gary Toward and Chris Henley's *Celebrating Teachers* is full of enthusiasm, fun and practical ideas to take away and put into practice. This fabulous collection of memories and stories is a celebration of the impact that great teachers have and an insight into the secrets behind their success. The book is a fitting tribute to the art of relationship building, excellent teaching and effective classroom practice – and a great toolkit of ideas and strategies guaranteed to inspire and motivate.

Paul Matthias, National Director, Hays Education

Having met the authors and read their previous books, it was with great excitement that I opened their latest work: *Celebrating Teachers*. From the outset, I was inspired – and immediately I thought of ways in which I could use this book with the staff in our school. The book shares a series of powerful testimonies from those who have been inspired by teachers who went the extra mile and tapped into the infinite potential of children's minds.

It shares timely reminders of the importance of humour, finding time for pupils and building relationships. Add to these the key ingredients of calmness, a variety of teaching styles and techniques and thinking outside the box with unfamiliar or less exciting content to be covered. I also love the notion of 'boomerang lessons' – those lessons that pupils want to come back to.

The authors are non-judgemental and provide encouragement for the reader to reflect on their own individual style and techniques. Many of the arguments they make are well known, but equally we need these welcome reminders – for example, that interesting lessons lead to higher levels of engagement and fewer problems around behaviour and concentration. We all benefit from frequent refreshment in order to keep the main thing the main thing. It is easy to become so distracted that we lose sight of rich areas of focus. This book helps us to remember, to celebrate and to enjoy.

In teaching we need the variety, idiosyncrasies, fun and enjoyment that each teacher brings to the classroom setting in their own unique ways. We also need the unrelenting commitment and positivity shown by the overwhelming majority of school workers. They keep the system functioning and, often in the face of adversity and criticism, inspire the children in their care. The power of the teacher should never be underestimated, and this book helps to remind us of this universal truth.

Liam D. Powell, Head Teacher, Manor High School

Chris Henley talks about 'boomerang lessons' – i.e. those lessons that pupils desperately want to return to. I would describe *Celebrating Teachers* as a boomerang book which is essential reading for teachers, at any stage of their career, and a good read for everyone else too. I read the book with a smile on my face, knowing that the teachers chosen are just the tip of the iceberg – there are so many other wonderful teachers, all of whom work tirelessly for their pupils. This book leaves you inspired to be a better teacher, and the checklist at the end offers an excellent summary of all the traits that help you to do just that. An uplifting and, at times, emotional read.

Pippa Procter, Primary Course Director, Durham SCITT

Celebrating Teachers shows exactly why teaching is a wonderful and rewarding career. It shines a light on real teachers, their tireless and motivational work, and how they make a difference every day to so many. The teachers in this book, some of whom I have known personally, are inspirations in many different ways and have inspired thousands of pupils over many years. And teachers, irrespective of different governments, policies and their directions, will continue to do just that. This book is for all those game-changing teachers we are lucky enough to have in our education system.

Tim Sutcliffe, Chief Executive Officer, Symphony Learning Trust

Gary Toward and Chris Henley

Celebrating Teachers

Making a Difference

Crown House Publishing Limited
www.crownhouse.co.uk

Published by
Crown House Publishing
Crown Buildings, Bancyfelin, Carmarthen, Wales, SA33 5ND, UK
www.crownhouse.co.uk
and
Crown House Publishing Company LLC
PO Box 2223, Williston, VT 05495, USA
www.crownhousepublishing.com

First published 2021.

British Library of Cataloguing-in-Publication Data
A catalogue entry for this book is available from the British Library.

Print ISBN 978-178583556-8
Mobi ISBN 978-178583578-0
ePub ISBN 978-178583579-7
ePDF ISBN 978-178583580-3

LCCN 2021939163

Printed and bound in the UK by
Charlesworth Press, Wakefield, West Yorkshire

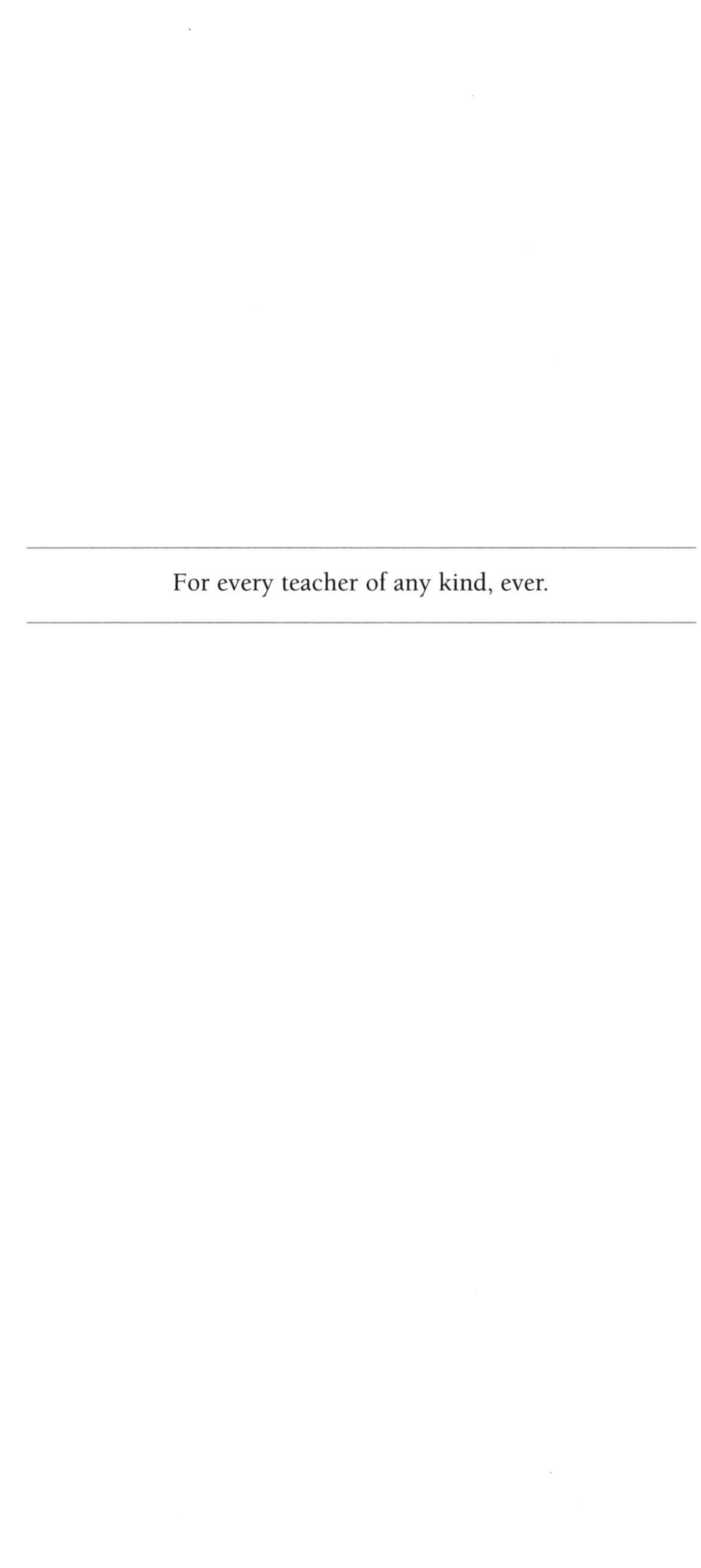

For every teacher of any kind, ever.

Acknowledgements

We'd like to thank the following people who nominated the teachers featured in this book and gave us fantastic insights into their personalities and classroom practice:

- Nigel Boyd
- Bob Cox
- Nikki Booth
- Ben Sperring
- Jade Derbyshire
- Meldin Thomas
- Paige King
- Dave Chapman
- Jean Smith
- Constantina Katsari
- Mandy Smith
- Isla Laking
- Mike Bushell
- Christopher Small
- Vladimir Mafaldo Grandez
- Alix Lewer and Dominic Glynn
- Nick Butter
- Jay Boucher
- Bethany Oaten

And special thanks to the following people who have helped us with additional valuable material or support:

- Tracey Townsend, Lincs Inspire Ltd, North East Lincolnshire Archives Office
- Steve Buckland for additional information about Mr Hope
- Martin Towers
- Warren Franz for the photograph of the teenage Dominic Glynn
- Mike and Sally Butter
- Vince Preston for the photograph of the adult Meldin Thomas
- Vanessa Haines Photography for the photograph of the adult Dominic Glynn
- 'Lindsey School, Cleethorpes Memories' Facebook group
- 'This is Cheadle Staffordshire' Facebook group
- 'Harrogate Granby High School Pupils '79–mid '80s' Facebook group

---

And to all brilliant teachers everywhere.
Thank you for changing lives for the better.

Foreword by Ben Bailey Smith

God, I must have been a real pain in the backside at school.

At 14, I knew I was smart, but I was way more comfortable procrastinating or mickey-taking. I was a one-trick pony – if it wasn't English or drama, the best a teacher could hope for from me was hour-long daydreams, silently staring out of windows thinking of girls and poetry, or poetry I could write to impress girls. At worst they would get pure old-fashioned disruption. I wasn't a bad kid by any means, but *boy* was I annoying.

Having gone on, as a young adult, to spend a decade as a youth worker, I quickly saw how smart kids could be a problem if they weren't *engaged*: emotionally and intellectually invested in the subjects they studied. I loved youth work – and still respect and support it from afar – but I knew it wasn't my calling. When I left the profession aged 29 and stepped onto a stage to tell stories to strangers in the hope that they'd laugh, there were no coincidences in play. You could trace that bold decision back to a handful of individuals whose words and actions left indelible prints on my imagination, knowledge, self-esteem and self-belief.

The first were a winning couple – two history teachers, both black – a man named Mr Lyle and a woman named Ms Dauphin. They both had a remarkable way of pulling my head out of the clouds and into the importance of appreciating where you are as a direct or indirect result of what had come before: the Second World War, in which my own father crawled into an infamous 77-day battle via the beaches of Normandy; the Windrush that brought my mother's family to the UK; the impersonal politics that created the hostile environment of the early 1980s into which I was born.

It all felt thrilling and relevant and suddenly I was looking forward to a Year 9 class that *wasn't* English. Looking back, the poignancy of the subjects they covered was really only half the reason. It was their passion, their belief and their energy, their thinly veiled firmness on us black boys who, statistically, struggled in inner-city areas, that made me sit up and take notice. I'm pretty sure that's why historical documentaries are my favourite kind of programme to this day.

I wish I could say it improved my grades as well, but that's another story that we don't need to disappoint my mum with again right now.

What it did immediately inject in me was the importance of focusing on the things that thrill you. I went into my English and theatre A levels with renewed vigour and determination. In English in particular, my teachers Mrs Barton and Miss Jonas knew that I wanted to do well and so would never let me slack; they were on me like a rash and the approach was super effective. I found myself wanting to impress them, wanting to make them happy, wanting to be praised.

Friendly pressure is good for me – I procrastinate without it. No one has forced me to write this foreword, which means you're kind of lucky to be reading it – I was *this* close to making a sandwich and rewatching the whole of *The Sopranos* instead.

The motivational ability of Gary Lyle, Helen Dauphin, Mich Jonas and Anne Barton mirrored the attention of other strong adults in my life – people I didn't want to disappoint. I try to be the same with my teenaged daughters when it comes to maintaining their focus, although I will quickly lose all parental intensity if they suggest alternatives to work such as s'mores and Marvel movies.

It's strange how transferable knowledge and skills can creep into your brain without you noticing it. It's like beautifully tailored inception – you just can't see the seams. I simply thought I was 'blessed', 'lucky' or 'talented' when I moved from stand-up to acting, to screenwriting, to children's novels ... But if I dig a little deeper, it's easy to see the link: where I inherited the confidence to express myself and my stories through writing or performing.

It's no surprise to me that my wife is a teacher. The good ones still inspire me; they invoke a romance and a nostalgia that has crept into my subconscious with so much verve that I went and married one. I come home every day from my various silly showbiz jobs and there she is at 8, 9 or even 10 pm, still grafting, preparing or debriefing, unable to go to bed until she's unlocked the puzzle of a difficult kid in her class, or created a foolproof lesson plan for the morning. I've seen her take time out of her own private life to visit vulnerable kids at home. I've seen her risk her own health during a global pandemic, all just to give these kids the invaluable gift of consistency. She will not rest until every one of her 30 pupils are up, on their feet, learning, contributing and smiling. It's unreal to watch from my cushy position of chauffeured cars and fresh fruit plates by the illuminated mirrors.

There's still a myth floating around that teachers knock off an hour and a half earlier than the rest of us, swan about during their numerous holidays, pocketing cash until the next 30 *whoevers* come through the gates in September. I'll be honest – I *wish* that were true. If it were, my wife and I would have real leisure time in-between my gigs to watch movies and drink cocktails, shoot the breeze … But, like the vast majority of her peers, she's fully *invested*, 24/7, and not appropriately remunerated for it in my opinion, but that's a different point.

This point here is about that *investment*. The returns on it are profound – it cannot be measured in quality or quantity. It's deeper than that. Positive engagement of our young people should be the number one focus of any nation. I mean, let's be real – it's not me and you and all these other old farts inheriting this world, is it? So, yes, why not? Let's celebrate the people who continue to have a small but significant hand in creating more good guys from the ground up, because I'm telling you – only the good guys can save us.

Thank you and God bless you all.

And sorry for that D, Mr Lyle.

It's technically still a pass, though.

Ben Bailey Smith

Screenwriter, actor, comedian, author and rapper[1]

1 Familiar to many as Doc Brown, his stand-up comedy stage name.

Foreword by Sir Anthony Seldon

In my years as a head and vice chancellor, I met a few teachers who thought they were 'inspiring'. But I met many more who did not think that they were inspiring, or sufficiently inspiring, and wanted to do something about it. That's why they were great teachers, and that's why teaching is a great, if not the best, profession.

This is evident throughout this important and timely book. The best teachers, and you will read about them here, are constantly challenging themselves to be better. They will be as eager to learn on their last day in school as they were on their first. The self-satisfied teachers, as is true of the self-satisfied everywhere, do not think that they have anything to learn.

There is indeed no better profession than teaching. I had a privileged education at an elite boarding school and an elite university. Barely any of my friends and associates would have considered a career in teaching, and although they never told me to my face, they rather looked down on me for doing so. The old jibe 'those who can't do, teach; those who can't teach, teach history' was never far from their minds (I taught history).

Looking at them now, as many of my contemporaries from school and university are beginning to retire, I sense a common factor: a certain emptiness in their lives. Their occupations – as lawyers, accountants, bankers and businesspeople, or in roles across the media and advertising – might have been financially rewarding, but were also often devoid of deep meaning and significance. They are unable to say, as we who have taught can say, that they changed the lives of thousands of young people for the better.

In almost no other profession do people willingly work long hours without demanding extra pay. The pages that follow are full of examples of the difference that teachers make, partly because the young people know that they care about them. Teachers stay on after school, they arrive early, they work long into the evening, they work at weekends and during the so-called 'holidays'. Why? Because they're inspired to do good and because they care. A professional lifetime of doing good and caring helps make them into the people they are. Those in other professions will rarely do anything extra without charging for it. Teachers have their reward – and money-watchers, equally, have their own reward.

Society still does not properly recognise teachers, in status, respect or material recompense. In terms of pay, it will never reward them as fully as they deserve. It does reward surgeons and other medical specialists. Surgeons open up bodies and save lives. Teachers open up minds and inspire better lives. Books like this will help to make teachers feel that their lives matter. In my experience, because teaching can be hard, lonely and tiring, we need to be constantly reminded how much we matter.

I would defy any teacher, would-be teacher or anyone who has opted for another job but who is thinking about teaching, even if only as a remote possibility, not to be uplifted by this important book.

Sir Anthony Seldon

Contents

Introduction

If you have to put someone on a pedestal, put teachers. They are society's heroes.

Guy Kawasaki[1]

Chris started teaching in 1979 and Gary in 1982. Between us we've been around the block. Ten schools, three headships, two deputy headships, 70 years of teaching and leading in schools across England. It has been a rollercoaster, but mostly one with incredibly satisfying bends, bumps and climbs, and only the odd cavernous drop. We have loved teaching. It has been our passion and will forever be so. For us there is nothing better than when you walk into a classroom or assembly hall to be greeted by a sea of faces which awaits your input. To have the platform to inspire, or to share your enthusiasm for your subject, is a huge honour. Not every pupil,[2] of course, buys in straight away, but that's part of the deal. The challenge, the reason for being there, is to take each and every one of your pupils on a journey to new places and new opportunities. To ride the sunny uplands of the mind, help pupils to wonder and instil them with awe. To furnish them with knowledge and skills that will help them achieve some, if not all, of their dreams. The fact that some of our former pupils have been kind enough to say that we managed that for them has been a wonderful reward over the years. You don't become a teacher to get rich. It's not the sort of job you do because you know that you'll very soon be able to buy a mansion or a flash car. You do it because of something that's more important than money: a desire to create change, to make a difference.

Since we hung up our chalk, whiteboard markers and electronic pens, it has been our privilege and joy to pass on our experience to the next generation of teachers. Our business, Decisive Element, has taken us all around the UK and into Europe, and our award-winning and bestselling books have circumnavigated the globe. In our presentations to trainee and newly qualified teachers (NQTs), we often ask them the question,

1 Quoted in Jason Fell, Guy Kawasaki: no 'secret sauce' for tech success, *Entrepreneur* (1 June 2012). Available at: https://www.entrepreneur.com/article/223691.

2 Throughout the book we'll use a variety of terms to describe the young people we teach, including 'kids' as it's a common term.

'Why are you getting into this job?' We acknowledge the challenges that they will face. Not every pupil will play nicely and do exactly as you want them to do, not every parent is fulsome in their support, not every newspaper is flushed with praise for the profession, and some of your friends might think you enjoy a 9am to 3pm working day and 13 weeks of holiday a year, which you spend sitting on a beach drinking sangria and soaking up the sun in between dips in a cobalt blue ocean. Oh, and then of course there's the government, the Department for Education (it's had various names over the years), her majesty's inspectorate and whoever is the current secretary of state for education all sticking their oars in. They all have a say in the ever-changing and turbulent world of teaching. But almost without fail, our fledgling teachers always come back to us with answers that make us instantly proud of them. They tell us how they want to make a difference, to share their passion for their subject, to help young people, to pay back the support they had. None tell us that it is for money; it is nearly always a moral or ethical reason that led them into the profession.

We believe there are many people who go above and beyond the call of duty in their chosen field, but there are not many professions in which people work extra hours for free. We cannot imagine many folk saying, 'I'll nip in on Saturday morning to help out,' knowing there would be no monetary benefit. We are being a bit tongue-in-cheek here, but we do believe that there are not many other professions in which the highly trained professional will turn up on a wet Sunday to help run the school Christmas Fair, or spend a week away from their loved ones leading 50 teenagers on an educational visit. Every teacher that goes into the profession knows that this is part of the deal and that they will not be paid for doing those things when they occur out of normal school hours. We have been in awe of our colleagues over the years. At one point, when we taught in the same school, we could count over 100 clubs and activities that went on each week during breaks, lunchtimes, and before and after school – all run by teachers and support staff for free.

And there's another thing. We're using the term 'teachers' but we're also talking about teaching assistants, lecturers, learning support assistants, librarians, and so on – they all teach. They all make a difference and share that common raison d'être of changing their pupils' lives for the better. They, in the words of Guy Kawasaki, are 'society's heroes', far too often unsung and – like our medical colleagues – far too often criticised, when, in fact, they are busily going about their daily role, making differences that will have long-term and often life-changing effects.

This book tells the story of those heroes by looking at a snapshot of what goes on across the UK – across the world, in fact – in our wonderful profession. It has often been said that medics save lives, that they heal people, and we agree. What a wonderful thing. It must be amazing to be able to do that. Teachers have a similarly important role; they make people. During the school years, up to the age of 16, we estimate that a full-time school pupil will spend around 16,000 hours in the company of teachers, which is almost identical to our estimation of time spent 'at home'. However, there's a difference. Time 'at home' typically isn't spent in the proximity of parents or carers; kids play with friends, go to clubs and do things away from their families. But at school they are constantly under the gaze of teachers. It's a huge responsibility, as parents are putting their trust in teachers to help build their kids.

If you have ever seen us present, you will know that we are a great fan of the story that retired professional footballer Ian Wright tells about his primary school teacher, Mr Pigden. In fact, the power of the impact made by his teacher is instantly demonstrated in Ian's autobiography, *A Life in Football*. The dedication reads: 'For my teacher, Mr Sydney Pigden'. Wright goes on to explain that he was 'the first positive male figure I had in my life.'[3]

Ian Wright tells us he had a chaotic childhood, that he'd do anything not to have to go home. Finding that positive male role model was the catalyst to his future success: if Mr Pigden 'hadn't worked to put me on the straight and narrow, I wouldn't be the person I turned out to be.'[4] When someone saw Ian Wright the child, instead of the challenging behaviour that he sometimes displayed, his future life would be transformed. Ian explains how one of the simplest interventions made such a difference to him. Mr Pigden simply took the time to sit down and talk with him. If Chris and I had a pound for every angry pupil who we'd scooped up from a classroom over the years, who said to us of their teacher, 'They just don't listen!', we'd be very rich. Mr Pigden defused that issue with Ian, who freely admits that he was an angry

3 Ian Wright, *A Life in Football: My Autobiography* (London: Constable, 2016), p. 82.

4 Wright, *A Life in Football*, pp. 164–165.

young person with 'full on rage'.[5] Yet Mr Pigden cut through that and formed a positive relationship with the young Ian, using what his pupil was good at – football – as a foundation. As Ian says:

> *He did so much for me as a footballer, which helped me elsewhere in life – he taught me about playing for the team, how I needed to pass the ball to other people. That was all part of him showing me how to communicate properly.*[6]

Mr Pigden may well have only been Ian's teacher for a relatively short time at primary school but his impact has been profound and long lasting. Surely there can be no better legacy than when you have used your skills to create positive change that transcends your own lifetime and has a knock-on effect on others.

That situation is no better summed up than by an anonymous letter to *The Guardian*.[7] Very sadly, a parent writes to say thank you to a teacher who has recently died, leaving a legacy of overwhelming positivity. The writer thanks the teacher for not only being inspirational for her child but also for the wider ranging benefits that came from the relationship – something that every anxious parent would want.

> *You made parents feel as cared for as our children.*

It's an emotional read, not just because it's evident that there was great sadness at the passing of this wonderful teacher and that it was incredibly hard for the parent to tell her child that his teacher had died, but because you gradually realise that because of this one teacher, many other children will benefit. The author of the letter, you learn, is also a teacher and was inspired professionally by her child's teacher, adopting techniques she saw having an impact on her child and their peers. They communicated something even more powerful than that: a vision.

> *In the short time I knew you, you taught me about the type of teacher I aspire to be.*

5 Wright, *A Life in Football*, p. 82.
6 Wright, *A Life in Football*, p. 83.
7 Anonymous, A letter to … the teacher who inspired my young son, *The Guardian* (11 April 2020). Available at: https://www.theguardian.com/lifeandstyle/2020/apr/11/a-letter-to-the-teacher-who-inspired-my-young-son?CMP=Share_iOSApp_Other.

On BBC One's *The One Show*, the actor Sir David Jason explained that Jason is not his real surname.[8] It is a stage name he chose when he came to register with the actors' union, Equity, as he discovered that there was already an actor called David White – his real name. It was then he remembered his English teacher, who had enthralled him with many a book, in particular one containing the story of Jason and the Argonauts, and so the surname Jason was chosen.

The teachers that we are looking at in this book are mere humans, but in all cases they seem to have superhuman abilities. Like sporting greats such as Muhammad Ali, Jesse Owens, Billie Jean King and Tanni Grey-Thompson, who transcend their sports for a variety of reasons, teachers can do the same and affect lives beyond the classroom and well into the future. There is no clearer way to see that than when a teacher inspires one of their pupils to follow in their footsteps.

The reason why both of us became teachers is because of teachers. We had totally different upbringings yet were each inspired to teach by a teacher. There is no history of teaching in either of our families. Chris comes from a long line of naval officers; Gary from a long line of coal miners. Chris was expected to join the navy to carry on the family tradition and Gary saw teachers as being on a social and intellectual pedestal so high that he never even thought he could join them. For both of us, to take a step to the side and develop a passion for education took quite a spark. And for each of us the fire was lit differently.

Gary's story

In July 1972 Gary ran out of the back door of his junior school, darted across the playground and leapt over the stone wall into the adjacent field. There he sat, back against the wall, sobbing. It was the last day of the summer term and he was leaving to go to grammar school, having passed the eleven-plus. His years of junior school hadn't been all plain sailing, but he'd loved it like a second home. He'd had some lovely teachers who made the sun shine in their lessons, and one who seemed to take joy in hitting her pupils with a ruler and pulling their hair. Years later, Gary bumped into another ex-pupil of this teacher, who said, 'I went to her funeral. Just to check if she was dead!' Sad

8 BBC, *The One Show*. Broadcast 26 October 2020.

but true, and it illustrates our earlier point about how, when teachers make a difference, they never un-make that difference. This is why it's so important that the difference is a positive one.

Fast-forward past the sunny summer holidays (Gary only remembers having great summer weather as a child) and the newly uniformed Gary, complete with a woollen blazer and all manner of new pens and pencils, became a secondary school pupil. It was a grammar school, so supposedly a cut above, but it was an unbelievably violent place with bullying at every turn. Gary was shocked on the first day to see pupils with full hippy beards. As a small 11-year-old, the gulf between him and those in the upper sixth was huge. Very little inspirational happened in the way of teaching to light Gary's fire throughout the first four and a half years. In fact, the opposite was true. Gary went from loving junior school to disliking secondary school. School became just a step he had to take before he got to the world of work, and he did just enough to get by.

It still puzzles him today that the education system at the time (and, indeed, we still do this in some parts of the UK) tested kids at the age of 10 or 11 and separated them on the basis of that test into different schools. Many of Gary's friends went to a secondary modern school, having not reached the standard required for grammar school; Gary hardly saw them again. The illusion that the grammar school was better is also still puzzling, because other than a few teachers who did the odd thing differently, this was a school that seemingly had little ambition to get the best out of every pupil. Looking back, Gary feels that middle-class kids with well-educated parents were at a huge advantage at that school, as they had a history of educational success at home and if the teachers were not that inspirational, at least they had something to compensate. Gary had loving, intelligent parents, but both had to leave school aged 14 to earn a wage to help their families. They wanted the best for him, but did not understand how that worked educationally. Thankfully, today, both Chris and Gary feel that our teachers are light years ahead and more and more working-class pupils are inspired to raise their aspirations. Having said that, there's still a lot of work to be done in levelling things out.

Outside of school Gary played many sports and had a range of interests. One of these was being a member of the Air Training Corps (ATC), which saw him go gliding and flying. Having been born only 15 years after the end of the Second World War, he had always been fascinated by war stories and, in particular, the Battle of Britain. So, the combination of the thrills of being in the ATC and his vivid imagination led him to the conclusion that he should join the RAF and become a pilot. This meant working harder and stepping up. This he was prepared to do to achieve his dream. Halfway through his fifth year came a definitive moment: his interview with the RAF. Gary now looks back with amazement to think that he simply took the day off school to attend it. There was no link between school and the RAF recruiting office and no letter from his parents. He simply hopped on a bus to Newcastle. Safeguarding was a distant shore!

Excitedly, Gary stepped into the RAF office. This was to be the beginning of his journey to the skies. Twenty minutes later he left, his eyes blurred by the tears he was desperately trying to hold back. He'd failed. The first test was eyesight and whilst he had perfect vision, he did not appear to see in colour very well. He'd failed the colour blindness test and his dream was instantly shattered. You cannot be a pilot without good colour vision.

Back at school there were no careers pep talks. There was no support system. There was no plan B. However, sitting in a chemistry lesson – a subject he really liked, not just because it had practical elements to it but because his teacher was engaging, told stories, made the class laugh and seemed a bit different to the rest of the old-school tweed-jacketed and tartan-skirted teachers he had for other lessons[9] – he clearly looked a bit glum. Mr de Middelaer, with his sharp Mancunian accent (Gary remembers another pupil asking him if he was from Liverpool, which not go down well at all), obviously noticed this and asked where he'd been when he missed the last lesson. Gary told him what had happened, explaining that he had just had his dream whipped out from under him because he was colour-blind.

What happened next changed Gary's life as his teacher stepped back and said, 'Right, that explains why you keep messing up the titration test. You need a different indicator. I will sort it so you can use bromophenol blue.' O level chemistry, as it was then, had a practical test. One thing you had to do was balance an acid and an alkali to have a neutral pH. The indicator generally used was methyl orange. However, Gary, who was acing every other aspect of his practicals, could not get the titration test right. Mr de Middelaer has spotted the issue. Gary could not see the colour change, but with a different indicator he could

9 Other types of clothing were no doubt worn, but memories work in strange ways!

succeed. The effect was miraculous for Gary. Suddenly he was nailing every titration test and could go into his chemistry exam with confidence.

This moment – this one act of a teacher noticing something, asking a question, then finding a solution (literally) – changed Gary's life. In Gary's head, a message from a Disney song was becoming an embryonic idea: *'I wan'na be like you'*.

This one act, a spark in the dark, of a single teacher seeing a problem and creating a way forward changed Gary's life: the future teacher was born. Thank you, Mr de Middelaer.

Chris's story

Chris's story is different. His father was a naval officer, and the expectation was that sons of naval officers would be sent away to boarding school at the age of eight. There was no discussion about it, that was the way it was. Chris's home was in Tunbridge Wells in Kent and the school chosen for him was in Winchester, nearly 100 miles away. Chris has no certain recollection of ever having been to Winchester before that time. He had certainly never been to the school; he didn't know a single other boy or a single adult.

Chris's father had a distinguished career in the navy, and Chris was hugely respectful of him, but empathy was not his strongest card. Chris – as a little boy of eight – was absolutely dreading the day when he was to be sent away, away from his home, his teddy bears, his guinea pigs and everything he had ever known. His father came upstairs to say goodnight the night before, and said to him, 'I expect you are so excited. You'll probably find it hard to get to sleep.' Chris did sleep; he cried himself to sleep.

The next day Chris and his mother went up to London on the train and were treated to lunch in his father's club: uniformed stewards, oak-panelled rooms, crusty colonels in wing-backed chairs. Best behaviour was expected, even from a little boy who just wanted to cry. After the lunch, Chris was taken in a taxi (the one glimmer of something positive for the day, as they went over Westminster Bridge and Chris had never seen the Houses of Parliament before) and they arrived at Waterloo Station to join the school train. They were greeted by a very severe but quite kindly lady with a clipboard. She wore a long trench coat and stout brown shoes. Chris thinks she had a moustache, but that may be a figment of his imagination which has grown over the years.

Chris's parents had lost interest in him at this point as they bumped into old friends from navy days and Chris was left standing on the platform next to the rather fierce-looking clipboard lady. Then came the fateful moment when the train was due to depart. All aboard! You are probably imagining that Chris got a hug and a goodbye from his parents at this point. No. It didn't happen. He was manoeuvred into a seat next to the window, clutching his teddy bear and crying. The train pulled out from the station in clouds of steam – yes, it was that long ago. He spent the next hour and a half staring out of the window at the steam billowing out over the hedgerows, crying. Half an hour to Woking, half an hour to Basingstoke, half an hour to Winchester.

On arrival at Winchester the new boys were met by a tall man with wild, eccentric, white hair and they were shepherded into his car – a very dilapidated Morris Oxford estate. From certain memory, there were about six boys crammed into the car. Health and safety? Probably not! After a short journey of perhaps ten minutes they arrived in front of a cathedral of a building. It had been built, so Chris learned later, in the Victorian age as either a hospital or an asylum. Chris was taken in through the grand entrance and glimpsed the longest corridor he had ever seen. It stretched to eternity. He knew no one, he had no idea what would happen next, he didn't even know if there would be food, not that he was hungry anyway.

That first night he curled up in his bed, crying, and whispered in his teddy bear's ear, 'Looks like it's just me and you, Ted!' He cried for a week. Years later, Chris came across a letter from the headmaster's wife to his mother, written about a week after his arrival, reassuring her that little Chris had shown no signs of homesickness. The anger that this letter provokes in Chris even to this day is almost unfathomable. Chris was a broken, traumatised little boy.

Into this world stepped a young history teacher called Mr Maxse. Chris remembers vividly the first time he saw him. Masters were required to each sit at one of the tables in the dining room and supervise breakfast. As Mr Maxse approached the table, it was obvious that he was not a morning person. From the moment he sat down at the table, it was clear that he and Chris were going to get along. He was cool, he was funny, he was sporty and they shared a love of cricket. He had a Sunbeam Rapier, convertible, with red leather seats and square wing mirrors. Now that was cool. He also taught lessons to die for. Chris remembers doing the Second World War with him, and he would do the Winston Churchill voice for all those great speeches. Awesome. Chris was mesmerised.

The biggest thing, however, was on another level altogether. To use today's parlance, he 'got' Chris. He knew exactly where this little boy was at with his emotions. He gave Chris the only reason he had for staying in that barracks of a school. Chris's every inclination was to run away, except for the fact there was an enormously high fence all around the grounds and he wouldn't have known where to go anyway.

Mr Maxse changed Chris's life. He was his inspiration, his role model, his saviour and, as Gary said, the Disney song 'I wan'na be like you' resonated in his head. He wanted to be a teacher, just like Mr Maxse. Time and again, through Chris's long career, when confronted with a particular issue or problem, Chris would think, 'How would Mr Maxse have dealt with that? What words would he have used? What would his facial expression have been? What about his body language?' Mr Maxse had clearly discovered that age-old secret of getting people to want to do what he wanted them to do. That's really what behaviour for learning is about.

Chris has kept in touch with Mr Maxse throughout life. Indeed, Mr Maxse came to stay with Chris and his wife only last year. There have been many times when Chris has tried to thank him for what he did, but somehow he has never found the right words.

This book is for you, Mr Maxse and Mr de Middelaer. It is for all teachers who have had a profound impact on young people's lives. This book is an ode to teachers, a tribute to those amazing teachers who have transformed lives and who continue to do so on a daily basis. We salute you and we thank you.

Getting the most out of this book

So, we've told you our view about how amazing teachers can be and given you snippets of our stories, but where we are heading now is into the territory of other teachers. We have gathered stories about teachers who have made incredible differences to others' lives. We know there are tens of thousands more like these out there, but these few – we believe – will give you a flavour of the power teachers can have and hopefully suggest something to all classroom practitioners about how they can be *that* teacher for their pupils. Whilst our principal remit has been to focus on the business of education, we hope that there is wider interest here, with lessons for life for any of us.

We have learned a lot whilst writing this book. We had definite expectations about what we'd find hidden in the stories people have told us, and they surfaced with hardly a fight, but we have been startled and bewildered a few times and this had given us even more to share with you.

We wondered if it would be difficult to get people to tell us their stories and what people would think of us for asking. Two ex-teachers writing a book about how great teachers are. A couple of big heads, you could say, banging on about how good their chosen profession is. But the opposite has been true. We have had amazing support from a huge range of people. Our requests for stories have been shared and reshared worldwide in all manner of ways. From the simplest word-of-mouth requests and social media posts shared to interviews with the BBC.

The support has bounced into our inboxes. Some people just wanted to tell us that our project was a great and worthwhile one and something that was about time, as there can be so much negative press about schools and teaching. You know the trashy sort of thing you see in some tabloids and hear from the mouths of politicians whose sole qualification to comment is that they once went to school. Schools aren't good enough, not as good as they used to be, not up there with this country or that country, teachers get far too much holiday and leave school at 3.30pm every day. Really?

After all our years in schools, and in our new roles of providing training and inspiration to teachers across the land, we have seen, as you would in most professions, some poor quality. But compared to the vast majority of committed, hard-working, creative, innovative, giving and enthusiastic teachers we have known and know, who go well beyond the call of duty on a regular basis, the ones who don't shine are insignificant.

Interestingly, however, we have learned from the huge amount of information that came our way that even those teachers who may not be the best of their profession do also make a difference for some. We had several communications telling us that whilst a certain teacher was not everyone's cup of tea, they really made their subject come to life. Similarly, there were mentions of teachers who had clearly not ticked all of the superlatives we mentioned earlier, but made a significant difference for one child.

Sadly, great things don't always make the headlines, so this book aims to put that right. Having said that, just like the fantastic medical staff we have in the NHS, teachers have given us a lot of reasons to say thank you, not least for their efforts during the coronavirus pandemic lockdowns of 2020–2021. The NHS staff's efforts were obvious and heroic in so many cases and places, whereas it wasn't always obvious – to the general public – what teachers were doing. However, many were in schools every day teaching the children of key workers. Others, when not in school, were setting work and marking from home. Often this was happening whilst they were homeschooling their own children. We know a teacher couple with two children. Both are secondary school teachers with GCSE and A level classes and throughout the lockdown taught in school, taught online, set work, marked work, took part in online staff and safeguarding meetings, led their teams *and* homeschooled their own children. This incredibly intense juggling act is not an uncommon situation, but one that we haven't really seen portrayed in the media.

There are lots of stories we've not included in this book, mostly because we didn't have enough detail, or because the story was too like another. In this latter category, we could have written another stand-alone book: *Teachers Who Inspired Their Pupils to Become Teachers.* This category of inspiration was far and above the most common thread in our communications from would-be contributors and is in fact vividly evident in our training presentations. You'll see it represented thoroughly here. We often ask trainees to stand up if they were inspired to teach by a teacher: typically two-thirds of the group will stand up.

We've loved writing this book. It has been both uplifting and fascinating. We have a collection of amazing stories for you to digest but, also, we have teased the magic dust from each one and laid it out for you to breathe in. You should crack a smile, even a chuckle. One or two have made us cry. See how they grab you.

For each story, we've pulled out the key factors that made the teacher *that* teacher – the difference that set them apart – and hopefully you'll be able to grasp some of their brilliance for yourself. Also, at the end of the book we've included a checklist of all of the traits we've spotted, so you can use it as a guide to being *that* teacher for future generations.

You may find that this is a book you can read from cover to cover. Or, alternatively, you might dip into it, soaking up a chapter at a time, especially when you are in need of some uplift and inspiration. We hope these stories will vitalise you, make you proud of teachers, and, if you work in the classroom yourself, feel a little glow inside.

It hasn't always been possible to find photographs of those inspirational teachers, but where we have, we've included them too. Unfortunately, some of the images are of a certain vintage and, having been scanned from old photographs, are not the sharpest. However, they do still capture something important, so we wanted to include them nonetheless. We also regret that we were unable to track down any relatives of Basil Du Mont, John Hope or Dennis Tweedy in order to be able to ask for more recent pictures. If they happen to be reading this, please do get in touch so that we can try to redress the omission in future reprints of this book.

W. B. Yeats, the brilliant Irish poet, is alleged to have said, 'Education is not the filling of a pot, but the lighting of a fire.'

Whether he did or not doesn't matter, the sentiment is perfectly right. Teachers light the fire in kids and many light such big bonfires they burn for a whole lifetime.

Take a deep breath and meet the fire lighters.

Chapter 1

Mr Hope

It must have been like Groundhog Day for the young Nigel Boyd. His dad was in the RAF and his school life until the age of 13 was one of both constant change and repetition. By the time he'd settled into what was to be his final school, he'd already been to five others as his family followed his dad as he travelled the globe to different RAF stations. This was 1976 and schools were very different in those days. Lessons were very dependent on what the teacher liked teaching and any schemes of work would be largely unrecognisable compared to what teachers of today are used to. There was no national curriculum and schools therefore had carte blanche to teach pretty much what they liked and in whatever order suited them until pupils picked options for their exams and syllabuses kicked in. This meant that Nigel often found himself repeating things he'd already been taught and there's nothing much more demotivating than having to do the same thing over and over again. We can just imagine his face on hearing his teacher excitedly inform the class that they were going to start a new topic on the Romans when he'd already done it twice before. Differentiation hadn't made it into the educational lexicon either, so there was no chance of a teacher doing something completely different for Nigel. If that wasn't bad enough, the opposite could also happen. He'd miss vital topics and would suddenly be bewildered by a new topic as it relied on another one having been studied. He was demotivated, bored and going nowhere.

Nigel freely admits that because of this he became the class clown and was certainly underachieving. Mr Hope changed this – and what a perfect name. He became the first teacher in Nigel's school life to spot what was happening to Nigel and set about making him feel differently about school.

We wouldn't be surprised if you were thinking that Mr Hope was a young and trendy teacher who glowed coolness. Not at all! Nigel describes him as being incredibly ordinary, middle-aged, unfashionable, always seeming to wear the same sports jacket and trousers. There was nothing young or trendy about him at all, but he was popular with pupils all the same. His lessons, unlike many Nigel remembers, were always calm. This was the time of corporal punishment (which was officially banned in 1986 in state schools in England and, shockingly, in 1999 in public schools)[1] and teachers could always resort to physical punishment if they needed to keep discipline. But not in Mr Hope's lessons; they ran smoothly, not because he was a disciplinarian, but because he made them so interesting. Nigel cannot recall him ever raising his voice.

Interesting lessons were just the start. Mr Hope performed that magic trick of making his subject important and made sure that the way in which he taught his topics gave his pupils an understanding of why they were so important. He put the topics in context so the class always understood the point and how the concept might be useful to them in the outside world – and that's not always easy if the subject you are teaching is mathematics!

But it was another thing that really made a difference for Nigel: how Mr Hope made him feel. As Nigel puts it, he made him feel good. This is because of the focused way in which Mr Hope used praise and rewards, ensuring that when Nigel put his hand up and made a valuable contribution to a class discussion or when he'd worked hard and solved a mathematical problem, for example, he was praised. The result of this was that Nigel evolved from the pupil who was attending school but pretty much going through the motions to one who wanted to do more and developed a desire to do well.

The whole class benefitted from this approach. One of Nigel's favourite rewards was on offer at the end of term. Quite clearly Mr Hope was tuned in to the kid culture of the time. Monty Python, the Goodies and Spike Milligan were generating all manner of surreal and often irreverent humour. Tapping into this rich seam, Mr Hope would reward the group for their hard work. Nigel particularly remembers how he would read extracts from Spike Milligan books, which the group all loved and found hilarious. He was particularly adept at impersonating the crow's voice from the slapstick classic novel *Pukoon*, which, possibly because it was a little on the rude side, had the whole class in stitches.

1 *Schools Week*, When did schools ban corporal punishment? (25 January 2017). Available at: https://schoolsweek.co.uk/when-did-schools-ban-corporal-punishment/.

'Caw!' said the crow.

'BALLS!' said the Milligan.[2]

Gradually, due to being immersed in this incredibly positive classroom culture, Nigel transformed from being a pretty average mathematician to one of the highest achieving in the class.

> 'I remember being really proud when Mr Hope suggested that I, along with a small number of other pupils in the class, took further maths, as well as our normal O level. I went on to have Mr Hope for A level and continued to enjoy his lessons, achieving my highest A level grade in his subject.'

Nigel is very clear about the impact Mr Hope had on his life and explains that without his teaching, he would not have had such a successful and enjoyable career.

> 'He certainly made me realise I had more potential – and his excellent teaching ensured I got top grades in maths O and A levels.'

Nigel was lucky enough to have other inspirational teachers in PE. Being very sporty he loved the subject, played football, rugby and cricket for the school and got to county level in athletics – all due to the teaching and nurturing of his PE teachers, who he says often went well beyond the call of duty, personally driving him to athletics events. They and Mr Hope inspired him to want to become a teacher. Initially, because it was his first love, Nigel wanted to be a PE teacher but later decided on maths instead. He did a maths-related degree at university, followed by a maths PGCE. Without Mr Hope awakening the mathematician in him, he says that he does not think that would have happened.[3]

2 Spike Milligan, *Puckoon* (London: Penguin, 2014 [1963]), p. 21.

3 We were also contacted by Steve Buckley, who heard about the book and Mr Hope's inclusion in it. Coincidentally, he was in the same class as Nigel Boyd and went on to become a maths teacher due to the influence of Mr Hope. He reiterated, almost word for word, what Nigel told us about Mr Hope's inspirational methods. Steve is currently head of the maths faculty at Macleans College, Auckland, New Zealand.

Nigel began teaching in 1984 at the age of 22. Such was the impact of Mr Hope's teaching style and influence on him he often modelled his teaching style on the methods that had changed his own life so much.

As we have already mentioned, when we present to trainee teachers and NQTs we often ask why they have chosen this career path. Over and over again (and there are more stories later in this book) we find that teachers so often inspire others to become teachers, just as happened to both Gary and Chris. The legacy that this creates is huge as the inspirational brilliance of one teacher like Mr Hope then gets transferred to countless others.

In Nigel's case, it had extra power. Having risen through the teaching ranks to head of department, then deputy head, he became a head teacher at the age of just 35. Over the next 15 years he was the head of three different schools. He also had spells as a local authority advisor and Ofsted inspector (including being seconded as an HMI for a year). Now a self-employed school improvement consultant, he looks back and wishes he could thank Mr Hope for the inspiration he was to him and wishes that he had taken the opportunity to thank him back then. But the power of Mr Hope's legacy does not stop there. It has continued into another generation. One of Nigel's children – partly inspired by Nigel's love of teaching – is now a head of history, teaching in a secondary school. All this stems from Mr Hope having inspired the young Nigel, helping him develop a thirst for learning and therefore forge a new path in life that would lead to more and more children being inspired. Mr Hope's legacy lives on today.

Teenage Nigel

Nigel, present day

Mr Hope, c. 1979

The difference?

We couldn't have picked a better teacher to start with, not just because Mr Hope has a great name for a teacher, but because he resonates with everything we believe a great teacher should be, with a pedagogical approach that we guess inspired hundreds more kids. Here are the insights that every teacher can take away from John Hope's incredible approach.

Nigel makes it very clear that not every lesson he went to was calm and full of well-behaved kids like the ones in Mr Hope's classroom. In fact, he also points out that he was fond of a bit of larking about himself and would have continued doing just that if something hadn't caused a change to occur in him. In our careers, we have never met a pupil who has skipped back into a classroom the next day having had a detention for misbehaviour the day before. Back in the late 1970s, we guess that Nigel would not have suddenly become motivated to work harder at his maths if Mr Hope had wielded the slipper or screamed and shouted at him. The first question every teacher must answer for every child they teach is *why*? 'Why should I sit here and listen to you? Why should I be interested in this topic?'

WHY

Of course, kids don't always verbalise those questions, although we have heard them doing so! But we know they think those things because, after years of working with pupils from Key Stage 2 to Key Stage 5, they have told us. One of the best things teachers can do is find out what makes their pupils tick. Just ask the questions and they will usually open up and tell you all manner of helpful things to inform your teaching style.

Mr Hope did one simple thing. He made the subject accessible and he ensured the pupils knew just why they were doing certain things. Gary still has no idea why he had to learn equations in maths at school, but wishes he'd had Mr Hope as a teacher because he would have ensured he 'got it'. This is crucial in all subjects, but even more so as topics become more challenging or when you find a pupil floundering in an area. But, even better, Mr Hope's lessons were interesting and he used humour too.

We call this a boomerang lesson: one the kids want to come back to. Chris likens this to theatre visits. The first time he went to the theatre and immediately wanted to return was when he saw *The Lion King* in London. He was so wowed by the production that he would have gone straight back in and watched it again. Are your lessons like that? It sounds like Mr Hope's were. If the pupils you teach enjoy your lessons, then you are so much less likely to have fidgety kids, chair swingers and caller outers. Adding laughter in a relaxed manner and bringing your own sense of humour to the occasion is also a great tool. We're not suggesting you have to be a stand-up comedian, but being able to have group chuckle is great medicine.

BOOMERANG LESSONS

Mr Hope also brought something else into the classroom: kid culture. In his day it was Spike Milligan, but now it will be something completely different. Mr Hope used it as part of his rewards system, but we also know that by combining kid culture into the learning, there is a greater chance that your pupils will be engaged in it. So, what is the kid culture in your classroom? We ask this because it's not necessarily what you think. Age, stage, area, time and place all matter. Whilst presenting in Blackburn once we discovered that many of the pupils in a particular Year 3 class had a fixation with buses. 'Why?' We hear you calling. Actually, we have no idea, but what we do know is that if their teacher could use buses in aspects of their teaching they'd be onto a winner. From shapes in maths to describing a journey in English, the educational possibilities are there.

KID CULTURE

Kid culture changes over time, so our top tip here is to constantly do your research, find out what's hot in your class and incorporate it into your learning. Of course, it may not be that all the kids are into, say, *Doctor Who*, but you can differentiate using kid culture too, or use the majority to create an energy that draws in the others.

Mr Hope used praise to create change and positivity, to get his pupils to believe in themselves and their capabilities. We particularly like this aspect to Mr Hope's teaching methods as we firmly believe that using praise effectively is a dynamic and extremely helpful approach. We could write a book on the topic ... oh, we have! It's called *The Decisive Element: Unleashing Praise and Positivity in Schools*.[4] But let's have a quick look at what Mr Hope did.

PRAISE

The key thing about praise is that it adds a glow to the person receiving it. Who doesn't like a pat on the back? But, as a teacher, it can also be your enemy. Get it wrong and you'll have the undesirable effect of a pupil stuck in their comfort zone. Here are two examples:

1. That's a fantastic drawing, Salman. You are so talented. You always do lovely drawings for me. Keep it up.

2. That's a fantastic drawing, Salman. You've really put effort into your shading this time, just like we talked about. That's made such a difference. Well done.

Can you spot the difference?

4 Gary Toward, Mick Malton and Chris Henley, *The Decisive Element: Unleashing Praise and Positivity in Schools* (Carmarthen: Crown House Publishing, 2018). In it we share many more ideas about harnessing praise in your classroom.

In the first one the focus is simply on how good the art is and how good at art the pupil is. You could easily illustrate this in any subject. You're a talented footballer, writer, actor, etc.

The second picks out the effort the pupil has put in and, importantly, links that to the good outcome.

It's the latter that is key to your classroom and the catalyst in Mr Hope's transformation of Nigel's performance and attitude in maths. Nigel, if you recall, was showing up as a talented mathematician, but Mr Hope praised his efforts, making him feel positive and say to himself, 'I want more of this.' The key is to relentlessly find ways to link the effort your pupils put in to a positive outcome that eventually leads to them raising their game and consequently their longer-term outcomes.

It's not always easy to find the reason to praise for effort as some pupils are reluctant to engage. But that's where you create your magic kid culture lessons and apply some differentiation so that they have an opportunity to shine and you find a reason to praise them. Don't wait for it. Create it.

Here's a challenge for you. Look down your class list. Which pupils need to raise their game? What are they into? What's their kid culture? Target a few of your pupils and differentiate some work for them, creating opportunities for praise. Praise for effort and outcome. Repeat this, ensuring they get the link. It sometimes takes a while. Even better, create a culture in your classroom in which every pupil understands that in order to receive praise they have to work hard – that effort rules and brings rewards. Then ensure that you are focused on delivering it.

Chapter 2

Mr Du Mont

We love names. In fact, during our presentations we have been known to list some of the odd and wonderful names we have encountered in our years of teaching. There's no educational purpose to it, it's just for a chuckle. Mr Du Mont is no different and Bob Cox's incredible teacher from the first half of the 1970s stands out equally well as having an incredible name. Mr Basil Du Mont: he could be a detective in an Agatha Christie novel or a magician on a Victorian stage. He sounds like he should be a 'national treasure',[1] alongside the ranks of Sir Ian McKellen or Sir David Attenborough. What we do know is that he is a legend. How on earth could he not be with a name like that! It just suggests brilliance of some sort, and in Mr Du Mont's chosen field of English teaching, he was just that to teenage Bob.

Bob's school was a secondary modern. Which meant that if you went there you had already been judged 'non-academic'. As we have said, the system that politicians thought was best for state education at the time separated children according to ability at the end of primary school, judged purely by one exam: the eleven-plus. We could spend the rest of this book bemoaning the negatives of this system, but we'll skip that for now – apart from saying that if you went to a sec mod, as they were nicknamed, there was a good chance that you would do less well than had you gone to a grammar school. So, to have a shining beacon of a teacher in such an environment was a huge advantage to Bob.

> 'He chose to teach at a secondary modern, not a grammar school, and, for me, that just may have made all the difference.'

Mr Du Mont was not just an English teacher. He had clearly been recognised for his ability quite young and had already been head of English for some time when Bob arrived at secondary school. Anyone who knows secondary schools (and that's nearly everyone) will know what it's like as many hundreds of pupils change lessons or scoot off

1 A term used far too frequently in our view.

for break and lunch. The corridors and doorways can be a mass of hustle and bustle mixed with a variety of peripatetic teachers carrying boxes or piles of books as they head off to their next lesson. Many teachers, of course, have their own classroom and do not have to run the gauntlet of the corridors, but for those who do have to navigate the tide of bodies to get to their lessons on time, they often look like the White Rabbit from *Alice's Adventures in Wonderland*, desperate to get somewhere on time. Not Mr Du Mont! Bob describes him as calmness personified, rarely rushing or seeming out of control, moving sedately from lesson to lesson nearly always, as he remembers, with a striped blazer and a relaxed air. A striped blazer! If you were at that school, you would know who Mr Du Mont was. He would stand out like a beacon and, to many of the pupils, he would look like a man from a completely different world. Indeed, he was.

'Mr Basil Du Mont was sophisticated, polite, debonair and academic. Many of us needed that role model!'

His world was one of calm inspiration. His lessons were staged so that you could not help but be engaged and caught up in the ever-changing moods and varied activities that modern teachers see as part of the standard diet in their classrooms. In Bob's schooldays there were many lessons that consisted of dictation: you listened and wrote exactly what the teacher said, copying, colouring in and being talked at. Of course, no one will hold those teachers in the esteem that Bob holds Mr Du Mont. His lessons were active and exciting, kids were invited to become the teacher and to write on the board, to read plays aloud and partake in out-of-your-seat activities. At the time, it was quite normal for a teacher to be emotionally detached and formal, but Mr Du Mont's formality had a small 'f' and his teaching style balanced more regimented exercises with surprising changes of mood, which could include drama or discussions.

The modern version of this is VAK, which stands for visual, auditory and kinaesthetic learning. This varied approach meant that engagement was much more likely, even with those who didn't see English as their natural territory. Bob wonders whether maybe, in some subliminal way, Mr Du Mont may have been giving pupils glimpses of how culture, literature and questioning could be there for everyone, not just to feed a career but as a gift for life.

The impact of this atmosphere was that high expectations seemed completely normal. There was not likely to be an apology for anything being difficult, Mr Du Mont just exuded the confidence that the kids could tackle whatever he taught them. He took 14-year-old Bob's class to see Shakespeare. Bob, and probably most of the rest of the class, had never been to a theatre.

> 'It was a revelation and I've never forgotten it. We wrote reams after watching each play and it was an outpouring of ideas, fed by Shakespeare and a great teacher together.'

Learning went beyond Mr Du Mont's classroom with school magazines, play reading and more theatre trips, including an open-air experience. Back in the classroom Bob and his peers had to work hard but without stress or threat. There was an absolute acceptance that challenging literature was part of the deal. They hadn't heard of any of the texts before, so what would have happened without a great English teacher to open the doors?

One of the doors that opened for Bob was to sixth form. From a lad with aspirations limited by his peers and social status, Bob – fuelled by Mr Du Mont's expeditions into the unknown – began to think he might be able to do something different. At the time a new school block had just been built to accommodate the increase in pupils occasioned by the raising of the school leaving age[2] and Mr Du Mont had the opportunity to develop a new seminar room and sixth form library, both of which would have been groundbreaking in a secondary modern school.

Sixth form was a natural extension of his classes with the younger pupils and were full of talk, questions and enquiry. When he introduced the A level texts it was never with a suggestion of anything other than excitement and accessibility. He passed on knowledge where needed but there was an emphasis on wider reading and the pupils' responsibilities as learners. For Bob and his peers Mr Du Mont played Cupid, firing arrows of literary love at them, instilling them with the desire to work hard and embrace the texts they covered. This, of course, helped when it came to exams as studying for them was more of a joy and less of a chore.

2 Raising of the school leaving age, or ROSLA, happened in 1972 when the leaving age for secondary pupils rose from 15 to 16.

In truth Mr Du Mont's reach extended way beyond the sanctuary of his classroom. It wasn't just those who took to English who appreciated his influence and the impact he made. He was a superb house captain and ensured maximum participation in all competitive events. In fact, even parents were slightly in awe of him and his standing in the school community. This was someone who made a difference, not just to his own students but across the board.

The natural continuation of Bob's journey was to university, of course, to study English. The fact that this occurred after study in a secondary modern was particularly unusual back then. Catalysed by Mr Du Mont's teaching, a fire began to grow, lighting up Bob's road to emulate his role model. Looking back, Bob says it's easy to see further links between the influence of Mr Du Mont and his own subsequent career.

> 'I taught English for 23 years and was head of English at a comprehensive school for 13 of them. Whereas Basil took us to theatres, I also launched literary tours with my students, taking them around the UK on double-decker buses discovering Bernard Shaw, Arthurian mythology or Cornish writers.'

Following teaching Bob became a roving educationalist and consultant, seeing time and time again that the pupils who had the opportunity to gain knowledge through enquiry and questioning excelled. Eventually, he decided to put what he had learned in his career into words. He dedicated the first book of his award-winning Opening Doors[3] series to all his teachers, and the value of Mr Du Mont's lessons stand out in his philosophy.

> 'The legacy of love of literature is vital as it does just become a grades race otherwise, so the books take me back to those times in the 1970s when finding a personal voice was so natural and normal.'

---

3 We recommend English teachers of primary and secondary have a look at these.

Teachers such as Mr Du Mont often have an influence that spans generations and develop a unique status within the community. Bob, over the years, has bumped into many folk from his school – sometimes older by 15 years and sometimes younger by the same – who are linked by a common bond: the legend that is Mr Du Mont.

The teenage Bob

Bob with one of his books

Mr Du Mont, c. 1970s

The difference?

There's so much to like about Mr Du Mont and his approach to teaching. But there are some particular things we'd like to pick out for you that we think helped him to inspire so many young people.

Years ago, as a head teacher, Gary was seconded from one secondary school to another that needed a bit of support. There were lots of good things about the school he went to and indeed there were some wonderful staff, but there were also far too many kids who were doing well in other lessons but were just not engaged in learning in certain teachers' classes. His then deputy head put forward his hypothesis very bluntly: 'If those teachers planned and taught interesting lessons then they'd not have so many issues.' It wasn't rocket science but Gary decided to watch every teacher teach and, unsurprisingly, his deputy was correct. The teachers who seemed to have the most problems with their pupils were indeed teaching lessons that even the most diligent and compliant kids would find difficult to enjoy.

OK, we know you are thinking, we are teaching you to suck eggs here, but it is such a 'state the obvious' thing that it's easily forgotten. And it is indeed forgotten. We've seen teachers who have constantly been graded 'outstanding' become complacent and forget that the first direction on the road to being a decent teacher – let alone a brilliant one like Mr Du Mont – is to teach lessons that engage the kids. When we say it's easily forgotten, we also mean it's easily not given enough thought, for all sorts of reasons. But forget it at your peril.

ENGAGING YOUR LEARNERS

Mr Du Mont clearly taught lessons that engaged his pupils, but there was something more than just being a creative and engaging teacher in the mix. He understood that sitting in his classroom were a mixed bag of learners, and that these learners had already – by not passing the eleven-plus exam, which meant they had been sent to the secondary modern school – experienced a kind of educational failure. There are several arguments you could make here, not least that some of the pupils may have been less academic or maybe were not quite into their learning stride. Of course, one of the big arguments against selection or testing at that age is that learning is not linear and many pupils start to shine a few years later. Bob is a great example of that. The key thing we think Mr Du Mont did was to teach lessons that suited a range of different learning styles.[4]

4 We talk more about learning styles and their validity in Chapter 10.

There are different schools of thought about whether we have different learning styles, but in our lengthy experience we have come to believe that children do learn differently. Some prefer to work in groups, some alone, some learn better if movement is involved, others tune in to rhythm and sounds. Some are visually stimulated by images and video, others prefer the written word. What Mr Du Mont did was to create a classroom in which lessons involved an ever-changing sea of learning styles. There was formal writing going on, out-of-seat activities, role play, drama and reading in various forms. This, coupled with his calm but clearly charismatic style, meant that his pupils bought into his brand of teaching and learning – and because of that the door would open for them to new and exciting experiences.

Teachers have the opportunity to weave webs of magic in their classrooms, to immerse their pupils in new experiences and leave them in awe of the things they become part of. The very best teachers sculpt these lessons like an artist would, pouring creativity and unique qualities into their work to draw their kids into a compelling world of learning. It certainly helps to have a passion about your subject – a desire to pass on your love of what you teach. Although, of course, not everyone likes everything, so sometimes teachers need to be actors too, portraying that enthusiasm even if they are not entirely fans of that topic themselves. Chris remembers going to watch a teacher deliver a lesson to a middle set many years ago. This teacher was one of the best teachers in the school but the lesson was completely lacklustre. The kids were twitchy and there was none of the usual magic in the air. Afterwards, Chris discussed this with the teacher, who responded by saying, 'Well, it's not my favourite topic.'

EVERY LESSON MATTERS

For us as teachers, we must look like we are super excited to be teaching every topic. If you're a maths teacher and not a fan of teaching fractions, you have to get your Equity card out of your pocket, pop your game face on and ooze enthusiasm. If you look like you're enjoying it and excited about the topic, then you've got a much greater chance of getting more reluctant learners into your tent. Mr Du Mont quite clearly did this and lit up his classroom.

Chapter 3

Mrs Brandow

One of the sheer joys of compiling this book has been reading about all the different reasons why teachers have been nominated. Some are giants of the profession, the lionhearts of their schools, who earn their places in school folklore by being larger than life. Others are cast from a different mould. We called our first book *The Art of Being a Brilliant Teacher*[1] and there have been times, when we have been on the road talking to audiences, that we have been challenged on this. Brilliant? Isn't that setting the bar a bit high? Can't we settle for half decent? Anyway, how do you define brilliant?

One of the definitions we often use involves the '30-year teacher', the teacher who kids – by then of course well and truly grown up – want to make the effort to go up to all those years later and say, 'Hello, remember me!' and tell them how they helped or supported them. Of course, we particularly enjoy doing this when we train NQTs because 30 years seems an eternity. At that stage of our careers, Friday was about as far ahead as we dared to look, but the years go by frighteningly quickly. We still have to pinch ourselves when we think about how between us we chalked up 70 years, but we still find it deeply humbling when apparently random members of the public come up to us by the broccoli in the supermarket to say hello and reminisce about the good times we shared together years and years ago in class. Sometimes it is hard to recognise them, whereas we, of course, are eternal Peter Pans who don't look a day older. We wish!

Memory lane takes us to different places; sometimes it is to the lofty peaks of excitement that were provided by school trips, shows or a particular stand-out routine in class, but there are other times when the impact teachers make is remembered in an altogether quieter way. It is an age-old truism of teaching that you never know what impact you have made. Chris was approached by a builder on the development where he had just bought a house. It turned out it was an ex-student

1 Andy Cope, Gary Toward and Chris Henley, *The Art of Being a Brilliant Teacher* (Carmarthen: Crown House Publishing, 2015).

of his who said, 'You were the teacher who listened to me when I was going through a rough patch.' It wasn't anything dramatic, but nevertheless this guy remembers Chris simply for listening.

Our next nominee, Mrs Brandow, is cast in this vein. Not a big character but someone who created that priceless commodity called time to help a young Nikki Booth. Nikki had made sound if not spectacular progress through secondary school, but he lacked confidence in his written English. Things came to a head in Year 10 when he received a series of low grades in his English coursework and exams, and was told plainly by his then teacher that he needed to improve the standard of his writing if he was to pass. Eventually he moved class, due to a reshuffle when that teacher left.

Enter into Nikki's life Mrs Brandow. She invited Nikki to attend some writing tutorials with her. These were lunchtime sessions, twice a week, when they would sit down together and look at how to improve his writing. Everyone who knows how busy the teaching day is knows how precious lunchtimes are. They provide a chance to stand back from the fray for a moment and take stock of where the day is going, never mind do the necessaries of grabbing a sandwich on the run in between tidying up from the morning's lessons, getting set for the afternoon, fitting in a quick phone call to a parent and/or taking a minute to touch base with a colleague. Phew! It makes us tired just to write this, let alone do it. So, for any teacher to forego that priceless breathing space is immediately commendable. The fact that Mrs Brandow did so time and again elevates her to a very special status indeed. There are not many who would do that.

> 'Mrs Brandow was the only teacher to openly offer to sit and work with me on a one-to-one, personal level.'

The sessions went on for several months in the run-up to Nikki's final exams. He will never forget the debt of gratitude that he owes to her for wanting to help him so much that she gave up her time for him. The outcome? A grade C in GCSE English, which would have been beyond Nikki's wildest dreams without the intervention and help of Mrs Brandow. Of course, success at GCSE is seen by 16-year-olds as an achievement of its own, but we always talked to students about GCSEs being one of the early pads on the lily pond enabling them to step across to the next chapter in their lives, opening up the windows of opportunity, with English and maths being key ones to get under your belt. Without Mrs Brandow, it is doubtful that young Nikki was heading anywhere across the pond. With his GCSE English safely under his belt, he went on to study A levels which took him on to university, where he studied music and Spanish, and, of course, essays were a key part of many modular assessments. He remembered all the things that Mrs Brandow had taught him during those lunchtime sessions about how to write well, and to this day he reckons that the advice she gave him helped him to secure the grades he achieved at university. Without her support whilst he was at school, what he went on to do would simply not have happened.

This young man, who had struggled so much with his English, has gone on to write successfully at master's level; he has written academic journal articles, book chapters and a full book, and he is currently writing 80,000 words at PhD level. He is in no doubt that without Mrs Brandow he would not be where he is today. Not only did she help him to lay the foundations for his own research and study skills, but the way in which she inspired him made him want to become a teacher himself. He wanted to do for others what she had done for him. Ten years into his own career and he is still inspired on a daily basis by Mrs Brandow. Of course, he has good memories of other teachers, but Mrs Brandow was the one who sacrificed her lunchtimes for him.

A recurrent theme of this book is what those who have nominated these fantastic teachers would like to say to them now. Nikki has not only gone on to enjoy his own successful teaching career, but he is a professional concert pianist, and classical music was a passion he shared with Mrs Brandow. When he gave his first concert at Fraser Noble Hall at the University of Leicester, he could not believe that Mrs Brandow was there in the audience. She had always enjoyed listening to him play whilst at school, and it meant the world to Nikki that she had come to hear him perform. His only regret? That she slipped away at the end before he could talk to her. How he would have savoured a chance to thank her so much for taking him under her wing during Year 11. He hopes that she would be proud of everything he has achieved as a result of her help. In fact, he goes as far as to say that he would play a mini concert, just for her.

The young Nikki

Nikki in 2020

Mrs Brandow

The difference?

We have spent years professing that developing positive relationships with pupils is a crucial role of the teacher. One of the key psychologists whose work supports what we know simply through years of experience is Gregg Henriques, who says that relational value is 'one of the most fundamental of all human motives' and goes on to explain that the extent to which we feel valued by those who are important to us is crucial.[2] One of the key aspects, he points out, is how much attention we are given from such a person – a teacher, for example.

RELATIONAL VALUE

In a nutshell, in every relationship we have, we yearn to feel valued, acknowledged and appreciated. This is hardwired into us, whether it be in personal or professional relationships. Chris's wife works full-time and Friday is 'cleaning day' in their house. After a morning of having his arm around the U-bend to ensure the sanitary ware is spotless, Chris purrs with pride when his wife inhales the pure air, tainted only with citrus fresh aroma, and says, 'Hmm, I love it when the house smells clean.' By contrast, spirits are known to dive when she says, 'You haven't done the kitchen cupboard doors.' It is the same in our teaching lives. One of the biggest gripes teachers have is when they feel they are working their socks off and no one is noticing, let alone giving them a pat on the back.

So, what about learners? What is clear here is that Liz Brandow dosed out helpings of relational value by giving Nikki her precious time. But that time was even more precious to Nikki. This was what made Mrs Brandow stand out. There were others who no doubt taught good lessons which Nikki enjoyed, but they didn't go the extra mile. In Mrs Brandow's case, she gave him her lunchtimes. Relationships don't have to be built in this way. It can happen during the natural interactions in a lesson, at the start as the class are entering or at the end when they are leaving. It could happen after school or before school. You don't have to dedicate a particular quantity of time, just the time it takes to make that difference. The important thing is that Mrs Brandow found a chance to look deep into her pupil's soul and make sure that he knew that she valued and rated him, and that with her help she knew he could improve. Quite simply, she believed in him and made him believe in himself in a way in which none of his other teachers did.

2 Gregg Henriques, Relational value: a core human need, *Psychology Today* (23 June 2016). Available at: https://www.psychologytoday.com/blog/theory-knowledge/201206/relational-value.

EVERY CHILD HAS HUGE POTENTIAL

She also believed he was improvable. It still shocks us to our core when we hear teachers say, 'I don't think I can achieve any better results with these kids.' What?! This suggests kids have a gauge which blinks in vivid orange letters to say 'FULL' when they reach the capacity of their learning. We think not. Bill Bryson tells us in *The Body: A Guide for Occupants* that the brain has an enormous capacity to hold information:

> *A morsel of cortex, one cubic millimetre in size – about the size of a grain of sand – could hold 2,000 terabytes of information, enough to store all the movies ever made, trailers included …*[3]

So, to suggest that a child can get to the point where a teacher can add no further learning is to do that child a profound injustice.

The best teachers are the ones who see the very best in every child – day in, day out – and who believe that every child is improvable. How easy it is to place a ceiling on kids' achievements. We have heard teachers say, 'I won't be tackling X with this set. It would be too hard for them.' Just as Mrs Brandow does, we believe that every child can learn and can make progress. We often use the analogy of the driving test. If you ask any class in a secondary school who thinks they will pass their driving test (an incredibly complicated and challenging thing to do considering all that gear shifting, indicating, mirror checking, braking, accelerating and much, much more), most, if not all, will put their hands up – and they are probably right. They will master one of the most challenging combinations of skills you can possibly imagine because they want to. They can see that it would be in their interests to do so and they believe that they can. Mrs Brandow never doubted young Nikki, and she made a difference that will last a lifetime.

3 Bill Bryson, *The Body: A Guide for Occupants* (London: Transworld, 2019), p. 50.

Chapter 4

Jane and John

Double acts are abundant across the cultural world. Ant and Dec, Ike and Tina Turner, Sherlock Holmes and Dr Watson, French and Saunders and Toward and Henley (just saying!), for example. But it's not so common to have that moniker in teaching. So, when we picked up this story from Ben Sperring, who'd listed his teacher as 'Jane and John', we were not quite sure what to expect. Would this be a double act in the classic TV comedy set-up with a funny man and a stooge? Would they be equals or opposites? How could they be one teacher? We know that job-shares exist, with teachers coming in on different days, so this is what we expected to find as we delved deeper. But, no, Jane and John were a proper double act and taught together in the classroom. Double inspiration! This immediately jumped out as something different. Jane and John taught Ben on the other side of the world in Shellharbour City, New South Wales, Australia.

Shellharbour City, like a lot of Australian place names,[1] seems to tell it as it is and doesn't keep you guessing about how it was named. But it's more than shells now, and apart from the awesome surfing and snorkelling opportunities, stunning beaches, diverse wildlife and beautiful scenery it seems to have nothing to recommend it at all! So, we imagine young Ben immersed in this environment outside of school; sitting in a classroom must have been a challenge compared to the lures of the great outdoors. But not when you have a world class double act teaching the new subject you've just chosen to study: earth and environmental science.

This was a new subject and the school had – as Ben puts it – 'zero resources', making a tough job even tougher for his teachers. There were no online resources either and no schemes of work. Coupled with the fact that only a few students had opted for it, Ben was uncertain about whether choosing this subject would be a wasted option and he wondered if they'd ever get to sit the exams. Luckily for Ben he had two passionate teachers who were prepared to invest huge amounts of time and energy into their small class.

1 Great Sandy Desert, Black Mountain and Pink Lake, for example.

For a double act, you need great teamwork and it seems this duo had it in abundance. John immediately sorted the resources situation. But he didn't just cobble together a few worksheets; he went straight in at the sharp end and invested a huge amount of time in writing a whole textbook for the course. Ben says that without that the class could never have seen the course through. John worked every night, every weekend and every holiday to complete the textbook. Every morning on the days he taught the subject, he'd photocopy the pages he'd just written to give out to the class, who'd pull out their folders and slip in the new pages. By the end of the course, each student had a full textbook's worth of material in their folders, including diagrams, tables, summaries and questions.

Even so, it must have been tough starting the course not knowing if there was a route to the end. However, Ben explains that Jane inspired confidence. Having had a life in industry, working for a steelworks before becoming a teacher, she'd seen the bad things we do to our world and had developed a passion for the environment and the science behind it. Her enthusiasm was contagious and spread through the classroom like a giggle in an assembly hall, infecting her students with her passion for and enjoyment of the subject she was teaching. She oozed positivity for the subject matter and, coupled with the support from John's amazing resources, Ben soon found himself looking forward to his new favourite lesson.

> 'Her enthusiasm was contagious and this quickly became the subject I enjoyed studying the most.'

Because of this, Ben has developed a lifelong love of science and nature. His career brought him to the northern hemisphere and he now lives and works in London, heading up a teaching school – London East Teacher Training Alliance (LETTA) – where, of course, he can pass on his knowledge about how inspirational teachers can change lives. He has never forgotten the impact of the lessons with Jane and John, and says that the fact that they both took time to get to know their students and sought to enthuse each and every one of them with their own love of their subject has meant that he has brought that ethos into his own work. He collaborates with a charity called Earthwatch to deliver environmental science to the trainee teachers he works with and to provide experiences that might otherwise not be available to inner-city children, extending the legacy of Jane and John.

The teenage Ben Sperring in Australia

Ben, currently director of teaching school LETTA

Jane Cobbin

John Berry

The rules around safeguarding and health and safety were different back in 2002, and today we doubt if Jane would be able to put on a barbeque for her students, but back then it was a natural thing for an enthusiastic and supportive teacher to do. This has left Ben with his fondest memory of his time at school. Of course, there was a hidden agenda. Jane lived on a large farm, where her students could see much of the science that they had been learning about back in the classroom in action. Revision sessions took place there too and John, of course, was part of the deal. What's more, Ben points out, is that all of this took place during the school holidays, so both teachers were giving up their free time. The fact that Jane's husband was the head chef in charge of the barbeque illustrates the commitment and passion that fed the teachers' desire to support their students.

Ben has never forgotten the lessons he learned, not just scientific ones, about how amazing teachers can change lives and care about their students as Jane and John did. It's interesting that the ethos of Ben's teaching school reflects this so well. We wonder if there are echoes from Shellharbour in there. Of LETTA, Ben says:

> 'Our mission is to train and develop outstanding teachers, support staff and leaders for future generations of children. We share a common goal, which is to provide an exceptional education and opportunities for the children and communities we serve.'

The difference?

When Gary was doing his teacher training he remembers being warned by his lecturer to make sure that he worked out the rules of engagement in the staffroom. One rule was simple: don't sit down until you learn which teachers sit in which chairs. In fact, Gary still chuckles thinking about another student on his course who was in the same school but hadn't heeded the warning and was very bluntly put in his place when a wizened-looking teacher, wearing a tweed jacket and sporting an immense beard, barked the order to get out of his seat. Gary's mentor told him later that the older teacher had been in the school 'man and boy' and thought he owned the place. He was the staffroom's resident mood hoover and any new initiative or strategy he instantly labelled a load of rubbish. Over the years, we've sadly come across several similar characters.

These teachers are definitely not from the same mould as Jane Cobbin and John Berry, who were clearly forged in positivity and washed with a can-do spirit. It can't have been easy to suddenly find that you're timetabled to teach a brand new course and then realise that there are no resources for it at all. It would wither a few folk or at least be the root of a good moan. But not our dashing duo; they got stuck in, John producing a textbook and Jane fizzing her enthusiasm and using her own farm to illustrate the concepts they learned about in class.

GREAT RESOURCES

Teaching can be a tough job at the best of times, but it is the people who see opportunities in the middle of problems that help light the fire for their students. Such people are also a pleasure to work with. Heads of department and senior leaders will value them and often pick their brains and seek out their thoughts before making changes. These are also the people who, in our experience, stick their heads above the parapet and say, 'Pick me' when it comes to professional development or career opportunities.

Furthermore, the kids value teachers who do things for them. Ben spotted the graft that John was clearly putting in by writing the textbook and worked out that if it hadn't been for his tag-team teachers, he would not have had a course to follow, let alone been able to go onto university. To craft resources for a new subject is no mean feat. And working from ground zero, John's investment in his students – to help open the windows of their mind – was huge. The easy option, of course, is to plod away creating a few worksheets. But some, like John, put on their magician's cloak and enthral their students with something new and different.

So, it was easy for Ben and his peers to buy in to their brand of education. No matter what age or stage they are at, kids will size up their teachers in some way and in their own terminology ask themselves, 'What's in it for me?' One of the ways in which great teachers answer that question – at least partly – is by letting the class know that they care about them and that their mission is to give their class the very best. That links back to the concept of relational value – which we touched on with Mrs Brandow – but, also, it's as simple as showing that you are prepared to invest time and effort in them. There's no hard and fast rule to say that they have to, but great teachers go that extra bit further because they want to.

WHAT'S IN IT FOR ME?

> *You always appreciate it when people stick their neck out to support you.*
>
> Nish Kumar[2]

2 Quoted in Aamna Mohdin, Nish Kumar gets frosty reception at Lord's Taverners charity feast, *The Guardian* (3 December 2019). Available at: https://www.theguardian.com/uk-news/2019/dec/03/nish-kumar-gets-frosty-reception-at-lords-taverners-charity-feast.

Chapter 5

Mr Dunford

We wondered whether anyone we had worked with personally would be nominated for inclusion in this book. When this story came through both of us were so pleased. If we could only name one teacher we both knew who we wanted to be represented here, it would be Stuart Dunford. We knew Stuart well. In fact, Gary worked alongside him as head teacher in two schools and was excited to appoint him to become head of mathematics at the school where we all worked together.

Throughout this time the school was evolving rapidly. There was a lot to do, many changes to be made and Stuart was a key player in the mix, constantly and consistently being a positive influence amongst his peers, a whole-school leader and a creative teacher who led his team by example. But it was his teaching and leadership in his classroom that stood out for the young Jade Derbyshire, when – back in 2013 – she joined his maths class.

Jade tells us how, at that point, she was failing at maths, a subject that she found boring, confusing and very difficult: 'My worst subject.' The feeling had begun at primary school and developed as she progressed into secondary. She gradually became convinced that she couldn't do maths and the more she said it to herself and her teachers, the worse it became, with one teacher assuming that her protests about not understanding were just laziness. This, Jade says, only made matters worse, especially when homework was set, as neither she nor her mum could understand it, so she often had tears and tantrums when she could not do the work.

So, heading into Year 9 and with GCSEs only three academic years away, she was not feeling very confident that she would get a decent grade in the subject and feared more of the same frustration. However, she found instead that she was greeted by a teacher who had clearly prepared for her arrival, having done his homework on her. He asked her what it was she didn't like about maths and what she thought he could do to help her, which was an instant confidence boost. This small but vastly important moment was then turbocharged by the time Mr Dunford took the time to listen to Jade and put strategies in place to support her. In fact, Jade tells us that this happened in every lesson

– he'd go out of his way to ensure that she understood what they were learning and what she had to do. She remembers how he would crouch down low to the level of the four girls sat on her table and go through the work with them in different ways, constantly questioning their understanding until he was sure that they had cracked it.

It wasn't all plain sailing, though, and Jade's lack of confidence would sometimes return. On one occasion it really got to her and she broke down in tears, completely overawed by the topic they were studying. Quietly, Mr Dunford suggested she went to the toilets to dry her eyes. On her return, she was met in the corridor by Mr Dunford who again listened to her as she described why she was upset – how stupid she felt amongst the others who 'got' maths. She'd always felt like this but Mr Dunford told her not to worry – that it was normal and that just because her peers understood the work quicker at some points it didn't mean she couldn't or wouldn't get it. We all learn differently, he told her, we all get to these things in our own time. Sometimes we just have to work harder at things that some people find easier. He convinced her that she *could* do it, sometimes employing tough love too. Jade remembers how he would walk around the classroom and ask pupils particular questions. She dreaded this and on one occasion was totally unprepared as she'd not got anywhere near finding the answer, automatically murmuring, 'I don't know.' Mr Dunford didn't bat an eyelid and joked, 'Well, I'm not letting you leave the room until you've tried to work it out and I don't mind if you're wrong.' Jade says that she sat and gradually worked out the answer before quietly saying it out loud. She remembers his exact words in response. 'Yes! Correct, Jade. I told you that you could do it if you put your mind to it.'

For Jade this was a moment of realisation. The ethos that Mr Dunford reflected in his classroom – more than any other teacher she had – was the ethos that was put to the pupils regularly in assemblies: effort matters. She became more and more confident, eventually volunteering to answer questions in front of her peers, without fear of getting it wrong. She began to enjoy the subject that for years had haunted her and was her least favourite, even to the point of looking forward to the next lesson. In fact, there was a wider impact. Prior to this, Jade's days would be clouded by maths lessons. Having the subject four times each week meant that there were four bad days, especially if she had maths last lesson. That would mean a whole day of anxiety as she gradually got nearer to her dreaded subject. By suddenly finding that she was enjoying and understanding maths, she enjoyed school more and also felt that it helped to unlock her potential in science, as maths was so important in that part of the curriculum.

It was this lesson that Jade tells us was the thing that changed her life. Looking back, she can clearly see that by giving her the confidence to know that with effort you would most likely succeed, but if you failed, you still learned lessons through the act of trying. Failure didn't matter, but putting in the effort did.

Jade remembers being sad when Mr Dunford told her that she'd made so much progress she was going to move up sets. She'd found a teacher who had inspired her and she was going to have to leave him to move to another class. Immediately worried, with her old demons having a poke at her, she asked him what would happen if she failed in the higher set. But she was immediately reassured as he reminded her that she should be proud that her hard work had resulted in so much improvement; she was on the up, she would succeed in the new class and she would be more than able to hold her own. What's more, the teacher she moved to, Miss Melvin, taught in the same style and also worked hard to support her pupils, finding different ways to make the learning fun and memorable.

Jade gained a C in her maths GCSE, a grade she wouldn't have dreamed of a few years earlier. She believes that Mr Dunford taught her, at a very crucial stage in her life, that she could really do anything if she put her mind to it and she has carried this with her since leaving school into everyday tasks and into her workplace. He taught her to believe in herself.

'He taught me not to give up so easily, to have a more can-do attitude and to keep trying even when I felt like giving up and crying.'

Jade looks back at the lessons she learned beyond maths skills and sees what Mr Dunford did for her as a catalyst for her success. She is now an office manager at a firm of chartered surveyors and points out that she would not have achieved this position at such an early age had she not possessed the self-belief given to her in those maths lessons. She remembers the recruitment process for the position and in the last interview, when the pressure was really put on, she was asked what made her think she could do the job. She was very clear in responding,

'I know I can do anything when I put my mind to it.' She was offered the job immediately afterwards. Later, she asked her director what had set her apart from the rest of the candidates and was told that it was her can-do attitude and ambition to succeed that stood out. The voice of Mr Dunford echoed in her ears. There is so much she attributes to his teaching and aims to apply aspects of it in her role as a manager. She has found the resilience, the bouncebackability, that she learned from Mr Dunford, which is a major tool in the ups and downs of the world of work. She remembers how, earlier in her career, she had worked in the office of a construction firm. She often found an underlying sexism in the culture there, with men telling her she couldn't possibly know something because she was a woman. She found this belittling, but was determined to prove them wrong and constantly fought back against that unpleasant tide.

Jade would love to tell Mr Dunford how he changed her life; she says she owes him a million thanks for helping her to be confident and happy in the classroom, for making what could be a boring subject fun – not just for her, but for countless others on whom she knows he had a huge impact. Sadly, neither Jade nor the two of us can pass this on as Stuart Dunford passed away in the summer holidays before Jade joined Year 11, after contracting a mystery virus.

What we do know and can celebrate here is that Mr Dunford was a wonderful teacher – a teacher who challenged and inspired his pupils to succeed through their efforts. He gave them confidence, made learning fun and created success for them. We would like to add to Jade's wonderful account by saying that Stuart, as we knew him, was more than just a great teacher. Gary feels an everlasting gratitude to Stuart for his support in the development of the school, backing everything he wanted to do, no matter how unusual it might seem. He was hugely respected by his peers, ploughed furrows in the corridors, dining rooms, yards and fields on duty, building relationships with pupils. He extended learning beyond the classroom with clubs, activities and trips. And, something Jade points out, he always had a smile.

Jade in her high school days

Jade today

Stuart Dunford

The difference?

It's quite clear that Stuart Dunford had a major impact on Jade's life and will do for many years to come. There are many facets to his lessons and qualities as a teacher that Jade described that sit happily alongside others we have written about in this book, but we'd like to highlight one area in particular.

Stuart listened and acted upon what he learned about his pupils. We guess every teacher could say that they listen, but in our experience that is not always the case. There's listening and there's hearing. Jade mentioned another teacher who just assumed that her assertions that she didn't understand were excuses and laziness. Stuart listened and sought to find a way past the 'shitty committee' in Jade's mind, which was constantly telling her that she wasn't good enough.

Listening and learning from what you have heard is a key skill for teachers. In the hustle and bustle of the classroom, the very best teachers can tune in to what is being said either directly or indirectly and act upon it: change based on reconnaissance. Stuart Dunford clearly had a strategy for doing this and by talking to his pupils and teasing out of them what their barriers were and seeking to find the tensions that stopped them learning, he could formulate strategies to support them. It's also quite clear that before teaching Jade he'd done some homework on his new class and knew who needed intervention and support.

UNDERSTAND YOUR PUPILS

In our careers as school leaders, both of us often had to scoop up young people of varying ages from outside classrooms when they'd been sent out. We have lost count of the number of times we've been told by the young person that the teacher doesn't listen. Of course, that doesn't necessarily mean that the teacher didn't listen. There are all sorts of different scenarios that may have played out before the removal of the pupils from the classroom, but, nevertheless, the pupils strongly felt that they were not listened to. In a classroom situation, there's a lot going on and typically when we told the teachers the pupils' view of the situation, they would assert that they had been listening. But did they hear? Did they act? Or did they assume that the fuss was just a misbehaving child?

Who knows exactly? But what is for certain is that Stuart Dunford was able to do more than say he listened. He would make sure that the pupil *knew* that he'd listened. Jade knew he had done so because he told her what he was going to do to support her and then acted upon it. That is full listening and is what *that* teacher does: the teacher who is different to all the others, the one who really makes a difference. Ensuring that the pupil feels listened to is crucial to developing the change that is needed for them to move forward, especially when – like Jade – they dislike the subject so much they feel totally hopeless.

LISTENING

The final step of listening was the action put in place. Gary remembers a situation in which he was told by a schoolteacher that the method she used to teach her class of infant pupils how to spell was 'look – cover – write – check'. Gary, not being the world's greatest speller (thank goodness we have autocorrect here!) asked what she would do if that didn't work. He was told that this was the method she used, and she would continue to use it. Even when challenged further the teacher stuck to her one and only method and refused to think that there might be many different ways in which you could support a child with their spelling. The very best teachers, like Stuart Dunford, seek to find different ways forward. Jade remembers that he would persist in trying to find a way to unlock the understanding that she and others in the class needed. She could see that a different method might help some but not others, and that Mr Dunford understood this.

> *When people talk, listen completely.*
>
> Ernst Hemingway[1]

1 Ernest Hemingway, *Across the River and into the Trees* (London: Arrow Books, 2004 [1950]), p. 171.

Chapter 6

Mr Dee

This next nomination takes us back to the days when it was still legal to cane children; in fact, not only legal but quite common. Memories of those days evoke extraordinarily strong emotions on all sides of the debate. Gary was in the back of a London cab a few years ago. He was heading for a keynote slot at a fairly prestigious conference in an exclusive venue, so he didn't want to be late. As cabbies do, the driver struck up a conversation with Gary, who let slip that he was a teacher. It was like lighting the touchpaper: out came a diatribe of this guy's considered thoughts on education. After all, everyone is an expert, aren't they, in so far as they have been to school themselves? (Even secretaries of state think that!) Clearly fond of the sound of his own voice, he climbed into his subject with a denigration of kids these days: explaining and bemoaning how much things had disintegrated since he was at school!

Gary kept his own counsel in the back seat, quietly ruminating on the fact that this guy was not a shining paragon of virtue, but, as he didn't want to be late and was aware that an unhappy cabbie can easily rack up a decent fare by taking a deliberately longer route, he decided just to let him run with his strongly held viewpoint. Once he had worked himself into a veritable fury at modern schooling, children and life in general, he turned to Gary – taking his eyes off the road momentarily as though the gravity of the situation justified it – and said, 'I bet you wish you still had the cane!' It was a statement, not a question. Fortunately, they soon arrived at Gary's destination, so time did not allow for a response.

As Gary went up the elegant steps to his conference venue he thought of all the things he would have liked to have said. He would have welcomed the chance to explain why he thought it was, in his view, a good thing that we have moved on from beating children with a stick if they don't do the right thing, or how he couldn't be persuaded that even one single child had ever been coerced into enjoying learning after a physical beating. Later that day, he decided to take the Underground rather than risk facing further wrath from his friend the taxi driver.

Young Meldin Thomas was at school in those dim and distant days when the cane was still used. He admits that he was no saint back then. In fact, he was getting himself into constant trouble during his first three years at secondary school. Nothing big, just silly behaviour and backchat for which he was frequently in trouble and had found himself excluded on more than one occasion. He was going nowhere fast. Then came the fateful day when he was messing around with his mates and he aimed a kick at one of them. He missed but caught the window instead, which, of course, smashed. Oh dear! More trouble.

He was sent to Mr Dee's office. Mr Dee wasn't the tallest or most well-built figure but he had an imposing presence. He would walk around the school with his sleeves rolled up and a serious and rather menacing expression on his face that made you stand up straight as he passed. Discipline ran ahead of him, moulding even the toughest of nuts into shape. In his office, he had a cane lent up against the wall. There was, however, another side to Mr Dee. He was a woodwork teacher in the creative design department. Meldin was not great at academic subjects; he found it hard to sit still and not get distracted but he thrived in PE and creative design. To Meldin, Mr Dee was one of the kindest and most considerate teachers. He always had time for Meldin and he did everything he could to help him. In his heart Meldin was mortified that he had been sent to Mr Dee to face the consequences of his misdemeanour. One of the few teachers whom he respected and who thought well of him was now going to have to administer the punishment he deserved for what he had done.

Mr Dee played his role to perfection. He made Meldin stand at the desk and then went to get the cane – he paused, cane in hand. Meldin was petrified. He looked at Meldin, drew back the cane and just as he was about to hit him, he stopped and said, 'You really don't want this, do you?' Meldin's path through school changed in that one small moment. The most impactful thing was the way in which he felt ashamed of his behaviour in front of the one teacher who he felt had rated him and saw the best in him. He knew he had let himself down and felt he had let Mr Dee down. It was a turning point for Meldin.

He worked hard during his last two years at that school heading into his exams. He got the grades he needed to go on to college. Years later he met up with Mr Dee at a school reunion: they caught sight of each other and laughed. Mr Dee was an inspiration to Meldin. Although he had a good family and plenty of encouragement, he had been set on an alternative route which was leading him nowhere. It took a teacher like Mr Dee to turn him around, not by threatening him with physical chastisement, but by showing him that he believed in him. Where others had given up on Meldin because of his constantly challenging behaviour, Mr Dee saw the good in him and made sure Meldin could see it in himself.

Meldin has gone on from there to get good qualifications and to make a success of his life. He studied recreation and leisure at college as he wanted to work in the fitness industry but when he couldn't find the openings he wanted, he applied to the police service. He failed the recruitment process the first time around, so got a job as a postman for four years. When the postmaster opened up a gym for staff, he asked Meldin to run it, which he did until a second chance to join the police service came about, at which point he was successful.

Meldin has now been a police officer since 1991. He's been a local policing officer and a member of the tactical support team, becoming the force's first Afro-Caribbean officer authorised for firearms. Having moved to become a specialist trainer at the National Police Training Centre, Meldin was promoted to sergeant in 2008, leading a neighbourhood action team which oversaw radical reductions in crime, seizing thousands of pounds worth of drugs and cash. He then became the team leader for East Midlands Collaborative Human Resources Service (EMCHRS) operations training.

Most recently, Meldin has worked as the public order safety tactical advisor for the Black Lives Matter (BLM) events in his area. He is very clear about his role in these matters:

> 'Whilst I did not support the idea of the gatherings during the COVID-19 pandemic, I completely understood the feelings and sentiment that had overwhelmed not just this country but people across the world. This [the police officer in the US who killed George Floyd] was an officer like me who instead of looking after a detained person unlawfully took his life. We are there to protect and serve; he does not stand for the same principles that I do.'

If he could meet Mr Dee again today, he would want to say thank you – thank you for not giving up on him and thank you for taking the time to understand that he wasn't a bad kid, just one who was trying to find his way and getting it wrong.

We're sure Mr Dee would be very proud of Meldin.

The young Meldin

Meldin the police officer

Mr Dee

The difference?

It has been our privilege to enjoy our careers as the white heat in the crucible of aspiration transformed our education system. The selective system, which in its day had been a huge step forward, made way for a comprehensive secondary system, bringing it into line with the most successful systems in the world. It was no longer good enough to provide an education with the prospect of good outcomes for a hand-picked minority. There was an appetite for widening the window of opportunity for everyone.

At the same time, society was changing. Gary's taxi driver friend was harking back to days when there was an assumed deference towards authority, and in schools this was reinforced by the threat of physical punishment if you contravened. Even when the cane was abolished in the 1980s, there were still those who relied on this assumption of authority for imposing their discipline. There was the assumption that kids should do as they are told, and face the consequences if they don't. The world around schools was changing and so schools themselves had to adapt, in our view, for the better. Meldin's work in the police service has changed: police officers cannot rely on any kind of natural deference towards their authority. Teachers, like all those who need to assert their authority, have to learn how to get others to want to do what they want them to do. In the long term that will prove to be a much more effective strategy.

GETTING THE KIDS TO WANT TO DO WHAT YOU WANT THEM TO DO

Jack Dee was well ahead of his time. He realised that thrashing a slightly wayward young boy with a stick was not going to change him. He already had a good relationship with the boy, established by using lots of positivity, built up over the course of time in his lessons. By communicating to Meldin that he didn't think he was a bad lad, and by continuing to believe in him despite his poor behaviour, he gained the respect which allowed him to make that crucial intervention. He could have resorted to implementing the school's behaviour policy, based on punishment, but he decided differently and the impact was almost immediate.

Even though the days of actual beatings have, thank goodness, long since gone, kids will still recognise the stereotype as it is regularly caricatured in all manner of media and they will associate some of their teachers with that aggressive rule-enforcer who threatens you with penalties if you don't do what you wouldn't choose to do, can't see the point in doing and probably don't think you are any good at anyway. Mr Dee unpicked that stereotype. Meldin was expecting to be beaten: that was what happened to naughty kids. But it didn't happen.

SEE THE CHILD, NOT THE BEHAVIOUR

How can we take a lesson from this and put it into a modern-day setting? Every school has an elaborate behaviour policy, often with a tariff of consequences for poor behaviour. The main objective for every response to poor behaviour has to be to reach a situation in which that child is less likely, rather than more likely, to do the same thing again. Maybe a punishment is the easy option, but will it make it less likely that you will be in exactly the same position next lesson? Probably not.

Mr Dee played Meldin like a violin. He set him up and manufactured a method to cut into his psyche using all those micro moments built up over time in his lessons in which he had fostered a feeling of mutual trust and respect. That allowed him, when the moment was right, to be the one person who could get through to Meldin and turn his school journey on its head. The key tactic Mr Dee used here was to make Meldin feel the need for change. Meldin only turned himself around because he wanted to. It was just that it was Mr Dee who made him want to.

Chapter 7

Mrs Graham

One of the early lessons that you must learn when you become a teacher is that, however small or tall the kids you are teaching are, they will become adults given the fair wind of fate. A golden piece of advice given to a young Chris was to ensure that no matter how frustrated you may feel, or how challenging a pupil has been, you should always seek to solve the problem with positivity. We've already pointed out that teachers make differences, and we'd love to ensure that every difference is a good difference, one that lasts a lifetime. As a teacher, you'll bump into current pupils, past pupils and a wide range of relatives of pupils who also know you or have at least heard of you. It'll continue happening for years after you retire too. We've met teachers who really don't like it when they become minor local celebrities who everyone wants to talk to when they bump into them at a football match or in the shops. It's not quite like being a major pop star and being mobbed at the airport, or having a gaggle seeking autographs as if you're the latest tennis player to win at Wimbledon, but it is a degree of fame. Frankly, we've always thought of it as an honour and confirmation that we must be doing something right if people wanted to come and pass the time of day with us. We always loved it when, on a Monday morning, a pupil rushed up in the corridor and said, 'I saw you in Asda[1] on Saturday.' The look on their faces was always a cross between astonishment and perplexion when we'd reply, 'Yes, I know, we spoke to each other!' It just highlighted how much the encounter meant to that pupil.

A step forward and another privilege is when your former pupils cross the bridge and become equals. It is a rite of passage. Old habits can often die hard: Gary recalls playing rugby alongside a former student who congratulated him on a crunching tackle with the words, 'Nice one, Sir!' rather to the mirth of everyone else on the field. A very special place is reserved for those former charges who go from poacher to gamekeeper and become colleagues, which brings us to our next nominee: Mrs Graham.

1 Other supermarkets are available.

Of course, that was her real name, but to a young Paige King she was always 'Mrs Sunshine'. By definition teachers only really know what is going on in a child's life between 8.30am and 3.30pm, roughly, every school day. They can often have very little awareness, with the best will in the world, of what is going on in the background. Over the years, your antennae can sometimes pick up the vibes, which may allow you to gently probe to see what information may be forthcoming. Sometimes you stumble across a backstory in conversation and other times you take the bull by the horns – where your relationship allows it – and ask directly how things are going.

Laura Graham was the primary teacher who was there for Paige in Years 3 and 4 when life was tough. Paige's parents were going through a break-up, which is an awful transition for any child to have to go through. We human beings fall in and, alas, out of love, and it is so hard to do this without causing collateral damage to those for whom we love and care. Paige remembers that both her parents were amazing, but it was still an awful time for everybody involved. Her mum was left with less money, and home no longer felt like home. She would watch her mum cry and it felt as though there was a constant raincloud over their house. She was envious of her friends' families and often felt the need to pretend that she was happy and to overcompensate for her own home life.

We wonder how many children we have taught over the years who have been going through all sorts of trauma at home for whom coming into school was a safe haven. Gary often talks about a light-bulb moment in his early career when it dawned on him that not everyone in his class looked forward to the school holidays, let alone Christmas. For many kids school is a chance to escape from unhappiness in the home, to enjoy a structured environment and, if you are very lucky, to have a teacher who values you and cares about you, and makes sure that you know it.

Paige remembers walking through the classroom door every morning and seeing Mrs Graham's face smiling. Legend has it that you can change a child's life in a moment with a smile or a kindly word. In Paige's own words, her world changed, instantly and dramatically. She felt like a child again. Mrs Graham would listen to her and would never turn her away when she needed a hug. It felt as though she had a glow of sunshine around her, hence she became, to a vulnerable young Paige, Mrs Sunshine. Even now when she thinks back to that time she feels a gorgeous warm feeling in her stomach – and this is years later.

Paige grew up in a deprived area and there was an acceptance that the chances were stacked against you ever moving away. However much your parents encouraged you, supported you and pushed you to be your best, the reality seemed to be that the die was cast and you were likely to remain in that area for the rest of your life. However, it was to turn out differently for Paige. She used to reflect on the impact that Laura Graham had had on her. She knew in her heart that if it had not been for Laura, she would have been just as unhappy at school as she was in her home life, and she realised that if she could have the same effect on other children that Laura had had on her, she would be successful.

That was the catalyst for Paige to decide to become a teacher herself. Not only that, but she set her heart on being a teacher at the primary school where she had been a pupil, so she would become a colleague of the inspirational teacher who had done so much for her: Laura Graham. Her driving passion was to show the children that with the right love and support, you can reach any of your dreams.

There is one further twist to the story. Paige had never told anyone that she used to secretly call Mrs Graham 'Mrs Sunshine'; however, it turns out that that's what other members of staff call her. She inspired Paige to be that teacher and absolutely loves the person who she is today. Laura Graham showed her the way to love and happiness through a really hard time and inspired her to be that teacher for a whole new generation of children. She taught her that to be loved, appreciated and valued is the most important feeling a child should have when growing up, and it will make you feel that you can conquer anything you put your mind to. When life is tough and a child's home life is going through turmoil, teachers have to step up and provide that role, and Paige is eternally grateful to Mrs Graham for doing that for her. She changed her life, forever.

There is, of course, a happy ending to this story. When Paige graduated, she bought Laura flowers and told her that, without her, she would never have become who she is today.

Paige during her time in Mrs Graham's class

Paige, having become Miss King, the teacher

Mrs Graham aka Mrs Sunshine

The difference?

Building positive relationships is a hallmark of brilliant teachers, a sentiment which runs through this book like a mountain road, and is our mantra. It is glib to say, but maybe it is worth scratching the surface a little more to see exactly how inspirational teachers like Mrs Graham make such an impression on young lives.

She knew what was going on in Paige's life. It can be temptingly easy to think you know the kids you teach inside out, especially when you have taught them for a while. Chris had a tutor group he thought he had grown to know pretty well over the course of several years. One day he conducted a 'secret letter' exercise, meaning he invited all his students to tell him something they wanted him to know. The results were a massive eye-opener. Kids revealed insecurities about their learning – such as fear of being asked to answer in class, a dread of seeing their work corrected in their book, anxiety about their spelling – and much, much more, including vital information about what was going on in the background – for example, a younger brother who had been diagnosed with a life-threatening illness, bullying via social media and, more positively, success in trampolining at a national level. The message is simple: never tire of finding out what makes your pupils tick. The better you know them, the more you can make a difference in their lives.

WHAT MAKES YOUR KIDS TICK?

Laura listened. We have referred to the importance of listening before, and most teachers will reckon that they are good listeners, but there is more to it than meets the eye, or should we say ear? Make time to listen. This is often hard in the hurly-burly of the school day. If it is just not possible, by all means defer the conversation to another time. Tell the child when you can give them your attention and stick to it. Kids are very forgiving: they will understand if you have to say, 'I can't do this right now but if you sit down here, I'll be with you in five minutes.' Of course, you will need to assess whether something is urgent or not, but, generally, providing you are as good as your word, they will accept that they might have to wait for you to finish speaking to someone else or ensuring that the resources are ready for next lesson. When the opportunity presents itself, do not assume that kids will know that they are being listened to. Tell them that you are going to listen to them, reassure them that you are listening and tell them that you have listened. Kids who have no experience of being listened to at home will not automatically register this, but once you have become the person who they know listened, you will acquire a new emotional status which guarantees you a special place in their esteem, in their heart and in their mind.

CREATE A FEEL-GOOD FACTOR

Finally, Laura made Paige feel 'warm in her stomach'. Almost all of what we know about the human brain has been discovered over the last 50 years or so. We now understand much more about the evolution of the brain, and in particular what scientists call the mammalian brain. One of the distinguishing features of mammals is that their young are born underdeveloped and very vulnerable. To grow and flourish they need to be nurtured with love, touch, nutrition and warmth. Even as adults we recognise that X factor that makes us glow inside when we feel safe, warm, loved and nurtured, releasing all those feel-good chemicals into the brain that drive away the blues. Paige talks a lot about how Mrs Graham stepped into the breach when she was feeling pretty unloved because of the misery at home. When she came into her classroom, she instantly felt her world change. Gold star teachers spin a web of emotional magic which makes kids feel good inside, and that is what Laura Graham did for Paige.

Chapter 8

Mr Chamberlain

There are certain peculiarities which are perhaps unique to the world of education, and one of them is the way in which staff may be referred to by their initials. Indeed, as you entered the profession in yesteryear, it was a rite of passage as a new recruit to see your initials being used for the first time. Chris remembers the first time he had a tutor group, CH1 – the 1 representing the first year at secondary school before we went for the universal Year 7, 8, 9, etc. A glance at the timetable would see those initials CH – usually written in pencil on a massive piece of paper in those days gone by – and perhaps they'd be on the one that every secondary teacher used to dread: the daily cover sheet which went up on the staffroom noticeboard in those halcyon days when teachers would be expected to cover for absent colleagues. Again, the covering teacher would be identified by their initials.

All of which brings us to our next nominee: Mr Chamberlain, known by his initials, GAC. As far as kids are concerned, there are yet more fascinations with finding out their teachers' first names. Gary recalls being taught French by a first-language French speaker, and he and all his mates were convinced that her first name was Mademoiselle. The finer points of French personal titles had perhaps eluded him. Interestingly, Dave Chapman, who wrote to us to nominate Mr Chamberlain, doesn't know his first name to this day.

What he does know, however, is his nickname. Teachers' nicknames are passed down through the generations – and where different members of a particular dynasty attend the same school, one of the rituals that will pass from each succeeding child to the next will be the sharing of nicknames. Chris reckons there is a whole other book to be written there! Mr Chamberlain was known to all the kids as 'Dogend' because he always enjoyed a fag at breaktime. Classic! Of course, nicknames are usually part of the secret code for the kids and never to be shared with teachers. Not so with GAC! One of Dave's school friends had annotated the staff list in his yearbook with all of the teachers' nicknames. Unfortunately, he dropped it outside the staffroom and the contents were shared amongst everyone. One of the ones they enjoyed the most was Dogend.

Dave Chapman's story goes back to the year 1959 when he earned a place at a prestigious Kent grammar school for boys, established in 1887. However, Dave grew up across the county border in Sussex. If you come from that part of England, it is all-important which side of that county border you live. It is hop-growing territory and local folklore has it that hops grown in Kent fetch a better price than those grown in Sussex – at least that is what Kent people say – and so it was with education in the 1960s. Those from Sussex who passed the eleven-plus were permitted to attend a grammar school in Kent and so it was that young Dave Chapman arrived as a bit of an outsider, having to commute seven miles across the leafy, rolling Wealden countryside to school.

Dave had had a bit of a preview of GAC. A sixth form prefect from the grammar school paid a visit to Dave's primary school as part of what we now call the induction process, helping to familiarise the next cohort with what they needed to know before they started at the school. This prefect described Mr Chamberlain as 'a kindly disciplinarian' who would encourage all his pupils to achieve their potential in terms of study and exams. On Dave's arrival at the school in September, GAC was his form tutor. He was a history specialist, but he was also what we would probably call a head of year now: the principal teacher charged with looking after the new boys. He also taught, in today's parlance, personal, social, health and economic (PSHE) education. Dave remembers him as not being in any way aloof or distant in terms of his accessibility, and he was an effective personal tutor who made a profound impact on young Dave in terms of both his academic and personal progress. In fact, Dave reckons that without GAC's input, he himself would never have gone on to enjoy his own long and distinguished academic career.

Dave was a Sussex outlander, starting out in that big town school with very few friends at first. He found it all intimidating, but GAC settled him in from the very beginning by helping him to succeed. History was common ground for them both as Dave's father, himself a First World War expeditionary force veteran who had served on the Western Front, had ignited such an interest in young Dave. GAC had an enormous gift for bringing out the enjoyment to be had from truly engaging with whatever topic was being studied. He had a way of narrating epic passages from history with a constant to and fro of question and response. His class doubled as his audience but also as his fellow actors, and he beguiled and fascinated his pupils in equal measure. Dave recalls going home and sharing with his dad poems by Wilfrid Owen which GAC had introduced him to with such empathy at school.

It was GAC the motivator that Dave remembers the best. Another boy remembers his exhortation to pupils whose exam results had just come through:

> 'You may think that you have finished but I've got news for you. Why didn't you get 100%? Quite seriously, chaps, with a little bit of extra work you can do a good repairs and additions job to the mark you already have.'

Any of those boys would have gone to the wire for GAC. Dave credits GAC with nurturing his self-belief as he entered secondary education. He set high standards whilst demonstrating the value to be had from putting in effort. He taught young Dave to take proper care, for example, with his handwriting, spelling and drawing, but his concern for his young protégé extended to the sporting and social aspects of school life as well. Cricket was an area of mutual interest and GAC encouraged and opened doors for Dave there too.

Success in the world of education is often measured by raw scores in exam results, but GAC's influence was much more profound than that. He taught Dave to realise how fulfilling it can be when you aim to know your specialism in depth, thereby broadening your horizons. GAC was a Cambridge graduate himself, although he never bragged about it, so high standards were second nature to him. He passed this on to Dave and when he himself was preparing for the Oxbridge entrance exams, GAC's influence was instrumental in bringing about Dave's admission to Cambridge to read modern languages.

One other thing Dave recalls about GAC is the way in which he could read Dave: he knew him inside out. He led a trip to the National Schoolboys Own Exhibition at Earls Court, and on arrival issued some fairly hazy instructions about the boys going around in groups and reconvening at set times for lunch and for their eventual departure. The exhibition halls were packed and, of course, Dave soon became separated from his pals – probably, he remembers, because he was absorbed for two hours by the postage stamps in the Stanley Gibbons booth. He showed up at the eventual meeting place a few minutes late, expecting something of a rebuke which would have ruined the day for him. Not at all: GAC greeted him warmly and humorously, alluding to the virtue of a free spirit and an inquisitive mind. Today's teachers will shudder at the laxity of health and safety and safeguarding procedures, but in those more innocent times GAC knew his pupil. He could read him inside and out and he could judge what was the most appropriate way to deal with the situation.

Dave fears that he has lost the chance now to say thank you to his inspiration and role model, but if he could have one last word with GAC, he would want to thank him for training him to be self-directing, especially in relation to study, and for expanding his horizons with such lasting effect.

A thoughtful young Dave Chapman

Dave, present day

GAC during his teaching days

The difference?

One of the gifts that the best of teachers possess is to be there for the children who don't quite fit the mould. Gary remembers interviewing potential PE teachers for a vacant post, and some of them seemed genuinely surprised that, whilst winning silverware to go in the trophy cabinet was always welcome and indeed valued by the school community, he was just as interested in how they would engage those kids who had no love of or aptitude for sport. Schools can be ruthless places, where the peer police amongst the kids patrol the boundaries of acceptable behaviour. If you don't fit in for whatever reason, you can be made to feel pretty miserable. GAC instinctively knew that Dave was an outsider. Most of the other boys would have known each other from primary school. Dave was from across the border, and GAC took him under his wing and made a difference in young Dave's life. Brilliant teachers are the ones who 'get' their kids, especially the ones who are a bit different. Sometimes it is a smile on a Monday morning or a moment when they down tools to listen which makes the difference – kids may remember those moments for ever. They can be a turning point.

GAC made learning come alive in the classroom. We have a long and detailed national discourse about how to improve educational outcomes for young people in the UK. We talk of structures and systems, inspection criteria and syllabus content, but it is teachers who are the decisive element. It is great teaching in the classroom which inspires and motivates kids to learn. The most common refrain from kids when asked why things are not working out in lessons is that it is 'boring'. Brilliant teachers are the ones who spin a web of magic in their classrooms, with lessons which inspire and enthral. Gary remembers watching a young English teacher reading a passage from his favourite book to one of his classes, and, of course, it being his favourite, it wasn't hard for him to inject an infectious passion into his reading, but it was what happened next which has stayed with him. He paused and waxed lyrically to the class (a not very able middle to bottom set) about why he loved that passage so much. He was able to pull out examples of metaphors, similes, onomatopoeia and eye-catching turns of phrase, and the kids were entranced. They had never given a second thought to the power of language before, and they set to their next written task with enhanced vim and vigour. Great teaching opens the windows of the mind, and, once open, they never close again.

BRING THE LEARNING TO LIFE

Finally, GAC was a brilliant motivator. Every teacher has to work out what it is that will make their pupils buy into their brand of education and 'Because you need it for your exams' is never going to get them rocking in their seats. GAC taught in a grammar school environment which, by definition, catered mainly for reasonably able kids, but even in this context doing just enough was not an option. GAC was very ambitious for his classes. He didn't just want them to do well, he wanted them to do really well, focusing relentlessly on the effort that they were putting in. It didn't matter which rung of the attainment ladder they were on; he wanted them to climb to the next one and the next. It can be tempting when planning lessons to play safe, but inspirational teachers are the ones who see talents and potential in the kids, who want them to take risks, to discover new frontiers and achieve things beyond their dreams. GAC set the bar high and made a lasting impact.

CHALLENGE THE KIDS TO RAISE THEIR GAME

Chapter 9

Mr Tweedy

If you're reading this and you're a teacher or training to be a one, you more than likely have a mobile phone. Not just any phone, though, probably a smartphone. In fact, you may well use your smartphone to do all manner of interesting things, like listen to music, watch videos, play games and even make purchases. When we started teaching mobile phones were science fiction! We both grew up in an era in which the idea that you could have a personal communicator was something that would only happen if you were on the Starship Enterprise in *Star Trek*. Gary's house didn't have a landline until he was 16, with the number 623. He remembers it being installed and proudly giving the number to his school mates (all of whom had had phones for some time). If you listen to him dreamily and wistfully blather on, you'd think he grew up in a black and white village that eventually had colour installed in the 1960s. And don't even get him started about old money, he'll give you his last shilling to tell you about it!

There was so much that was different about the world in the 1960s, but things were changing rapidly. The Second World War was well in the past, rationing had ended and towards the end of the 1950s the then Prime Minister Harold Macmillan told the country that we 'have never had it so good'.[1] There was a wind of change in the air and, in education, the transformation from the tripartite system of schooling to the new comprehensive system. Jean Smith was one of the pupils involved in one of the early pilots for the change and found herself at a junior high school as it transitioned from a secondary modern to a comprehensive school. That was complicated for Jean as she was expecting to do some GCE[2] exams and to leave at the end of her fourth year (now called Year 10), but suddenly she had an extra year ahead of her.

1 Rosemary Bennett, We've never had it so good: 1957 was the happiest year, *The Times* (24 January 2014). Available at: https://www.thetimes.co.uk/article/weve-never-had-it-so-good-1957-was-the-happiest-year-ctx8whpgw.

2 General Certificate of Education, the forerunner to our current GCSEs.

Her school life had already been complicated, largely due to home circumstances. Jean remembers the exact time she became involved in what must have seemed like a ping pong game of school moves. At 11.00am one day towards the start of her second year at the secondary modern, her father announced that he was leaving and going to sea with the Merchant Navy. Jean, who had lost her mum at the tender age of 3 was, at that time, living with her elder sister. Her father had remarried and had been living with his young wife and their two young children. Jean was expected to move in with her stepmother to help look after her half-siblings. This meant a change of school and the very next day she started at a new secondary modern, an hour's bus ride from her father and stepmother's house. The work at her new school was entirely different to her last one and, try as she might, it was a struggle to catch up.

Very quickly, though, the tide turned again. Her father came home for an extended period of leave and Jean was sent back to her sister's and her old school. However, this didn't last long as her father went back to sea so she was needed again. Another move!

It must be hard to imagine how Jean felt about this. She told us that she 'just got on with it', but it must have been tough moving between schools so frequently, with no continuity in her education. Having said that, Jean tells us that she actually loved being at school and didn't find the work hard, apart from maths. However, like lots of working-class young people, Jean left school at the age of 14, but only after promising her teachers – who clearly recognised that she could do well academically – that she would pursue her education at night school.

She left school during the Easter holidays and started work as a stock control clerk at Thomas Bolton's copperworks one week after her fifteenth birthday. Jean says she was a very young looking 15-year-old and describes herself as 4 feet tall and 6 stone. Being a new recruit, she started on the low wage of only £3.00 per week,[3] but was promised a pay rise if she could achieve her English GCE. So, it was off to night school.

It seems difficult to understand how Jean had the energy let alone the enthusiasm to go, but a promise is a promise, and of course there was the incentive of a pay rise. She attended night school after work four times a week. Monday for English GCE, Tuesday for maths, Wednesday

3 That's 60 shillings. £1 = 20 shillings. Decimal is so much easier!

for one hour of shorthand and one hour of typing, and Thursday for Royal Society of Arts (RSA) intermediate English. It was here she met Mr Tweedy.

Mr Tweedy taught Jean for both of her English classes and for the first time she had a teacher who made her excited about a subject. Jean was instantly engaged and looked forward to his classes.

> 'He made the English language come to life and I began to realise that this subject was not just a means to pass exams but would be fundamental in any future career.'

Lessons weren't just copying out of books and grammar, as was far too often the style in many lessons Jean had experienced before; they were different. Mr Tweedy brought a new life to the subject and Jean loved it. He told stories to illustrate the learning, he encouraged her to experiment with her vocabulary and, as we will find out, kindled a new-found confidence in Jean. Many of his stories were personal, things that had happened to him in real life and he used these to show his class how he wanted them to write so they engaged with their readers. Jean describes him as being very open and warm with his students, getting to know them well and helping them to relax into the subject matter.

Quite clearly Mr Tweedy saw something in Jean and after a few weeks he asked if she liked the idea of teaching other people. This was a lightbulb moment for Jean and when she thought about this question, she realised that she had been teaching her siblings for quite some time, without realising that it was 'teaching'. Her responsibilities when helping her stepmother had meant that she had become a 'teacher' at home. After finding this out, new opportunities were created for Jean. On Thursdays, Jean was already supporting other students who were struggling with the work but soon she found herself allocated a small group which she would lead. The response from the group was very positive and Jean realised that she was making a difference and helping others.

Interestingly, it was during these sessions that Jean met her future fiancé, who struggled with grammar and punctuation especially. She spent a lot of time supporting him, teaching him aspects of the syllabus that he didn't understand. Things didn't ultimately work out for the couple but Jean looks back fondly at the glow on her fiancé's mother's face when he passed his exam. She'd experienced 'making a difference' for the first time.

Mr Tweedy, still seeing a teacher in Jean, began to encourage her to seriously think about going to university to qualify as a teacher. She'd thoroughly enjoyed the mini teaching role he'd allocated to her and was uplifted by the success of her charges, but she also knew that university was not going to be possible as she needed to earn a living. This was sadly often the case for young working-class people of the time. There were no grants available to Jean and she could not afford to take out a loan to pay for university. It was a hard thing to tell her teacher that she could not fulfil the dream he had for her and she remembers how disappointed he was when she did so. Even so, like all brilliant teachers he found a way to look forward and sowed more seeds to support Jean's future. She remembers how he would praise her for her work in English and remind her that she had the ability to become a teacher, telling her that she should take every opportunity to make this happen in her life. After two years of night school, Jean, of course, passed her English exam and her employer was suitably impressed, giving her a pay rise of five shillings each week.[4]

As we said earlier in this book, teachers quite often inspire others to become teachers. So, you are probably expecting us to tell you that this is what happened to Jean. However, that's not quite how it panned out for her. Jean has had a hugely varied career, working in secretarial roles, as a landlady, as an instructor for the Youth Training Scheme (YTS) – using the skills Mr Tweedy quite clearly spotted – and in human resources. Mr Tweedy's faith in her and his advice followed her everywhere and Jean says that she often thought of him as she gained more and more qualifications, including a teaching certificate for the YTS. But for her the icing on the cake was when, at the age of 50, she achieved the dream he'd put into her mind 35 years earlier and went to university in Derby – not to become a teacher but to study human resources.

Jean remembers how daunting the idea of going to university was – and despite many family members trying to persuade her that it would be fine, she still worried. But it was remembering Mr Tweedy's faith in her that finally helped her to take the plunge. She remembered how

4 Let's just put this into context before we go further. Five shillings was the equivalent of twenty-five pence in today's money. At the time a loaf of bread would cost one shilling and six pence, or, in today's money, seven and a half pence. So, Jean's pay rise was worth roughly four loaves of bread.

he'd raised her self-esteem when she had very little and believed in her at a time when her life seemed full of twists and turns. Now, 57 years since she last walked out of his class, she knows that his impact has had a lasting resonance all her life and into the lives of her children. In particular, she believes that her love of English influenced her children's love of reading and that this, in turn, may well have helped catalyse her son's decision to become an English teacher.

Jean with her young son Christopher not long after finishing night school

Jean's graduation

Mr Tweedy

The difference?

We never get bored of telling trainee teachers that they will never know how much difference they will make in the lives of most of the kids they teach. That in many cases these differences might be small, but in some cases are life changing and life lasting. Dennis Tweedy never knew the long-lasting impact he had on Jean, how his words would drive her on and follow her through life, helping her to become the successful person she became.

We are guessing here, but we think that if we met Mr Tweedy and told him this story, he might shrug and look a little confused. After all, he was just doing his job, wasn't he? Yes, of course he was, but he was doing it in a way that made a huge difference to a young woman who needed a boost. He clearly spotted that, took time to work out how he could fuel her with confidence and did what the very best teachers do: he tapped into something he could see that Jean would succeed in.

LOOK AHEAD, SPOT POTENTIAL

This story has parallels to the one we told about Ian Wright right at the start of this book. In Ian's case, Mr Pigden used his love of football to engage with Ian. In Jean's, Mr Tweedy spotted that she had the ability to help others and gave her the responsibility to do so. How uplifting it must have been for her to suddenly be rewarded with the role of teaching others. In the previous few years she had been moved back and forth, her destiny seemingly in the hands of others. Suddenly, she was persuaded that she could be her own person, that she had abilities and that she would be able to make a difference to herself and others by using them.

Gary remembers when – and this is taking us back to the days when he lived in black and white – he was given the job of filling the class inkwells every morning in his final year at junior school. His teacher, Mr Dixon, was a disciplinarian: the man who did the caning in the school. So, Gary was a little afraid to be joining his class. At the end of school one day he remembers being asked to stay behind. Worried, he made his way to Mr Dixon's desk, who produced a piece of paper with a drawing Gary had done in the geography lesson that afternoon. 'You've made a fantastic job of this, Gary,' said Mr Dixon. 'As a reward, would you like to be the inkwell monitor?' Gary thinks he grew an extra inch at that point. From then on he was no longer scared of his teacher and took pride in having a role in the class. It was only a tiny thing but looking back Gary thinks that Mr Dixon could sense Gary's fear of him, so created the opportunity to break down that barrier.

The radar of *that* teacher is broad ranging; it seeks out opportunities to make a difference. It might be about how to find the key to unlocking new learning, to help a pupil understand a new concept or technique. The reluctant contributor might be engaged because the teacher has twigged that they have an interest in a pop band and used it to create a differentiated lesson. A lesson may be constructed deliberately to create an opportunity to praise a pupil in order to raise their motivation, self-esteem or focus. The radar could spot that a child is less positive and more withdrawn on Fridays and that could lead to a discovery that their home life at the weekend is less than rosy, opening up a possible safeguarding way forward.

This is not something that comes naturally to everyone, but it is something that every teacher can work at and constantly improve. The key here is to know your pupils. If you are a teacher, look down your current class list. (If you are aiming to become a teacher, this is something to try when you can.) What do you know about each pupil? What are they interested in? What is their home life like? How do you make them laugh? What is your relationship like with them? What do they not like?

DON'T FORGET THE QUIET KIDS

We've been around the block. We know that there are some pupils who naturally introduce themselves to you by the way in which they behave. These may be the cheeky chirpy ones, the chair swingers, the wrigglers, the shouter-outers, the grafters, the beautifully polite ones or the ones who are often late. But what do you really know about them? And, most importantly, what do you really know about those who do not introduce themselves to you through their behaviour? The ones who just get on with stuff quietly, who never put their hand up or do anything untoward. The ones who do what they have to do but never stand out for any reason. We call these 'grey kids'. Chris remembers taking 90 Year 9 pupils on a school trip to Paris – that was half of the year group. They'd been in the school for nearly four years at that point. Counting them once they'd reboarded the coach near the Eiffel

Tower, he saw a face that made him twitch. He'd never seen that face before and instantly wondered how a child had managed to sneak onto his coach and join his school party. Thankfully, before tackling the interloper, he mentioned it to a colleague who said, 'Oh, that's Jasmine, she's ever so quiet.' Somehow, she'd become a grey kid and Chris could not remember ever having seen her in school – in almost four years – despite his wide-ranging and ever-present role.

Jean could have been a grey kid. But Mr Tweedy used his radar to get to know her and create a way forward for her. That is a hallmark of a brilliant teacher.

Chapter 10

Mr Buraselis

Both of us can remember our first day at school and it was nothing like that of Constantina Katsari. On her first day at school in Athens in 1979, she might have expected to be taught how to sit up straight, to put her hand up when she wanted to speak and then to begin learning the alphabet. Not at all. This was a little different. Constantina vividly remembers the first thing her teacher taught the class:

> 'Do not pick up any of the needles you see in the school yard.'

We bet you took a breath in when you read that? We certainly did.

Constantina grew up in a working-class family with, shall we say, a colourful and chequered history, involving guerrilla fighting, prison and protests. Her father was a carpenter who ran a strict regime. As a young girl, growing up in a tough neighbourhood where drugs and violence were commonplace, she was rarely allowed out of the house unaccompanied. Education was not a family trait – survival was – but for the deeply inquisitive and strong-minded Constantina, education was a way out. Like Roald Dahl's Matilda she devoured very book she could get her hands on and read volumes of encyclopaedias from cover to cover, educating herself as much as possible with the aim of leaving home and gaining, as she saw it, her freedom.

After she passed the entrance exams to the University of Athens with distinction (coming 11th in Greece) she was determined to follow in Indiana Jones's footsteps. However, it was the realisation during her archaeology and history of art course that she had an aptitude for history, which led to her turning her attention to that field. Enter Mr Buraselis.

So many times in our careers we have found the need to point out that learning is not linear, nor is it limited to age or stage. This means that teachers can have an impact on a small child, an octogenarian or anyone in between. We are never too young to start learning or too old to stop. And similarly, there is no one way to learn. For Constantina, despite all her educational success, her moment of change was waiting for her as a young adult.

Mr Buraselis – professor of ancient history,[1] to give him his proper title – was a strict teacher. He had no fancy teaching methods but had a huge reputation for the detail and quality of his lectures. Constantina says that this appealed to her own way of thinking as he would 'cut through the fluff' and get straight to the point to illustrate the history he was teaching. His use of research inspired her and, despite his very formal approach, she was drawn to his teaching and enjoyed his support right through her academic studies.

'Mr Buraselis stood by me every step of the way and helped me navigate the treacherous waters successfully.'

What was different from other lecturers who hadn't caught Constantina's attention was that he had clearly worked her out. She'll tell you herself that she was, and still is, headstrong. She knows her own mind and speaks it, and when her mind is set upon something, she works extremely hard to see it through. He knew that and when, having moved to the University of Liverpool for a semester on the Erasmus programme,[2] she set her mind to studying more topics than the course allowed (six instead of four). Apparently, this was not the done thing and the director of the programme complained to Mr Buraselis, saying that she was likely to fail because she would be overstretched. Mr Buraselis defended her vigorously and challenged the director to see if he was right – if she would fail – by letting her try. Needless to say, Mr Buraselis knew his student and she achieved a first in five out of six topics. Constantina imagines that he would have been laughing 'under his moustache' at the time. He certainly knew his student well.

Constantina is clear that it was how he challenged her to always get the best out of herself that made the difference and lifted her to another level of academia. The way he did this was to guide rather than insist, and hopefully therefore to influence her in her career development.

1 Constantina tells us that the proper way to address him was as Mr, rather than Professor or Dr.

2 A European scheme helping students study abroad.

> 'His influence is evident in my writings and the choice of topics I studied.'

But, interestingly, he was clearly not a miracle worker, as there were some traits he could not change.

> 'He also tried to teach me diplomacy, but he failed there … and with my unruly character.'

From then on, with total backing from Dr Buraselis, Constantina buzzed through academia, volunteering at the National Research Foundation where she was initiated in numismatics and epigraphy.[3] That was a one-way route to a PhD, and she won a four-year scholarship to study at UCL where she completed a PhD in monetary economics. Two post-doctoral research fellowships followed: one at the University of Exeter and the second at the National University of Ireland, Galway.

Her first full-time permanent position was as a lecturer in ancient history at the University of Leicester, a post she was awarded in 2005. She stayed there, teaching and researching, until 2013, when another challenge beckoned. She turned her attention to entrepreneurship and founded several start-ups. Now Constantina is responsible for setting up programmes in entrepreneurship at the University of Leicester and other higher education institutions.

We have heard many people talk about their teachers with great fondness and appreciation. There are few that have such a depth of feeling as Constantina.

> 'He taught me everything I know in terms of methodology and writing. If he established a school of thought, I would probably belong in that. I took all his courses in the university, even if credit did not count for them. He is my academic "father" and he holds my respect and love.'

3 Yeah, we had to look it up! Memorise this for your next pub quiz. Numismatics is the study or collection of currency, including coins, tokens, paper money and related objects, and epigraphy is the study of inscriptions or writing.

Eventually, Constantina would become a colleague and a friend of her professor. He was best man at her wedding and back in Greece he is her neighbour, so the positive relationship continues to develop. She says:

> 'To my parents I owe the ζην and to him I owe the ευ ζην.'

But we'll explain that at the end, if it's all Greek to you!

Constantina, present day

The difference?

How a teacher teaches in, say, Reception is different to how they would teach in Year 6. The difference in age may only be a few years but the difference in social maturity is quite great. It's no different in secondary schools where the gulf between the fresh-faced Year 7s and the sixth formers is vast, so, naturally, there is a different style of relationship between teacher and pupil. It's no different here, and the formal lecturer–student relationship between Mr Buraselis and Constantina was, in her eyes, just right. He knew her well and learned how to get the best out of her by understanding that she would rise to the tough challenges he set.

It sounds simple, doesn't it? If it was, then all teachers would have to do is set tough challenges and we'd be flying. The key, of course, is to learn about your pupils and to understand fully how and how much to challenge them. We've come across kids who initially could not cope with any challenge at all and, equally, others that – like Constantina – are totally up for grappling with difficulty. And so many shades in between. With the reluctant students, start small, creating a specific challenge that, whilst you know should guarantee success, is not an obvious gimme for the pupil. It certainly doesn't work if the challenge is too easy. Kids will work you out and be less motivated. The key here is how you set it up, and, again, the key to this is knowing the pupil and understanding their learning style.

TAILOR THE LEARNING TO THE PUPIL

Before we go any further, we need to mention our views on learning styles. The scientific jury is out on this matter. The idea that each and every one of us has preferred ways of learning – some approaches that help us more than others – has been both in and out as a pedagogical truth. Our view of it comes simply from experience. We two have taught thousands of kids in different settings across England. We have had the pleasure of observing hundreds of lessons, analysing the learning in classrooms. We've written more lesson plans and schemes of learning than we'd care to remember. We've designed many individual learning programmes for specific pupils. From this experience, we have witnessed, in our view, repeated evidence to suggest that individuals learn in different ways and that some ways are more beneficial than others because they fit with that child's personality. If we were writing a different book, we'd elaborate much further, but just to get it off our chests, here's one example.

Ellie, a bright and intelligent girl, was struggling with her spelling, so much so that it was affecting almost every aspect of the curriculum. It got to a point where several teachers emailed her English teacher asking if there was anything they could do to help. However, the English teacher replied that she used the 'look – cover – write – check' method, which was well proven, and that they could also try setting subject-based spellings for Ellie to learn as homework. There was no improvement. The following term Ellie's English teacher left and a new teacher arrived. This teacher very quickly spotted Ellie's potential and set about learning more about her and developing their relationship.

She noted that Ellie was very creative: she made things, drew things and crafted things well. At the next parents' evening she suggested to Ellie's parents that they helped her in a different way, using fridge magnets to make the spellings, using cardboard letters to create the words on the floor (the teacher made a pack of letters from cereal boxes), or encouraging her to use her paints to spell out the words. Fast forward to the present day and Ellie has a degree in English literature and a master's in psychology. She has taught English as a foreign language in China, Spain and the UK. Her spelling is excellent. You may have a different view on learning styles, but, in our experience, they are real and worth considering.

If a pupil works well with peers, partner them with a positive problem solver. If they need clear and obvious steps, scaffold the learning for them. They may be a kinaesthetic learner, so get them out of their seats. You may choose to differentiate the learning to link it to something they are interested in and hook them into the challenge.

The creation of success through challenge, in our experience, can – if steered correctly by an astute teacher – allow success to grow and grow. This is, in the educational sense, the Matthew effect, a term first coined by the sociologist Robert Merton[4] and based on a New Testament verse (Matthew 25:29):

> *For unto everyone that hath shall be given, and he shall have abundance: but from him that hath not shall be taken away even that which he hath.*

Which roughly translated means that success is more likely to be followed by success when someone is supported by someone who creates opportunity for them.[5]

4 Saga Briggs, The Matthew effect: what is it and how can you avoid it in your classroom?, *InformED* (1 July 2013). Available at: https://www.opencolleges.edu.au/informed/features/the-matthew-effect-what-is-it-and-how-can-you-avoid-it-in-your-classroom/.

5 Of course, the opposite is also true.

CREATE OPPORTUNITIES FOR SUCCESS

This is what Mr Buraselis did for Constantina, and her CV echoes it loud and clear. His support continues to this day, many years since he was her lecturer. He became a lifelong mentor.

Back to the Greek words from earlier. As a Greek ancient history academic, Constantina is acutely aware of the legacy her country's forbears have given the world. Aristotle is considered one of the greatest thinkers in history, and he was the teacher of Alexander the Great, whose debt to his teacher was so great he was inspired to say: 'I am indebted to my father for living, but to my teacher for living well.'

Which, in turn, inspired Constantina to say: 'To my parents I owe the ζην (my life) and to Mr Buraselis I owe the ευ ζην (my higher life).'

Being compared to Aristotle is high praise indeed.

Chapter 11

Mrs Malcolm

We have always reckoned that, broadly speaking, there are two things which motivate people to join the teaching profession. One is a passion for a particular subject and the desire to share that passion and use it to inspire young people. The other is the theatre of teaching – some people just love it. It is being in front of a class of kids that makes the blood course through their veins, and the subject matter is secondary. The next teacher in our collection belongs to the first group.

The joy of watching a young person 'get it' can manifest itself in different ways. There can be a light-bulb moment when the penny drops and the mysteries of algebra, grammar or electrolysis are suddenly uncovered, or it may be a process which evolves over time. Chris has fond memories of the moment when his older brother successfully taught him to tie his shoelaces. Suddenly, the daily frustration and embarrassment of not knowing how to do a double bow were banished for ever. Life started anew. Eureka! English teacher Monica Malcolm's influence over the young Mandy Smith was more gradual and developed over time.

A study of how teachers gain and hold the attention of their classes could be the subject of a whole new book. There are many different styles, from the strict disciplinarian to the extroverts who seem innately to command the attention of the kids. When Gary started teaching, he was partly under the leadership of a super confident senior teacher who could halt the flow of the corridor, and hush it into abrupt silence, with the click of her stilettoed heels. She commanded instant attention from the moment she walked into a classroom, assembly hall or corridor. She wasn't harsh or unpleasant, but she had an aura about her and a confidence that persuaded the kids to respect her. Mrs Malcolm was not like this; Mandy describes her as an unassuming diminutive figure who wore glasses, had short brown hair and wasn't particularly feminine in the way that she dressed. Someone who would blend in and may well go unnoticed in the average street.

However, she had a different way with kids and made a deep impression on young Mandy. Mandy's class was, in her own words, 'very lively'. Some teachers relish the challenge of having some characters in the class, whilst others quake at the very thought. Mrs Malcolm was extremely patient, and all the while was deftly spinning her web of magic around her pupils. Sometimes it can be difficult to unpick all the constituent parts of this, but for sure it is multifaceted, like the mechanism of a clock, with a myriad of different interacting well-oiled components.

The first thing that stood out about Mrs Malcolm was that she taught really interesting lessons and Mandy always enjoyed them. At the time, she was steeped in the culture of Smudge and Chewpen,[1] which was the prevailing orthodoxy of the day for English lessons. This approach had bored Mandy to smithereens and she found such textbook-based lessons tedious. With Mrs Malcolm, they would work on projects (Mandy reckons that she has still got her war project folder) and at other times they would work on a book. She has fond memories of studying the novel *Nancekuke* by John Branfield, which had a big effect on her developing mind. Mrs Malcolm had a special way of bringing stories to life and Mandy credits her with kick-starting her love of reading and writing.

The real thing that stands out in Mandy's mind about Mrs Malcolm is the way in which she celebrated kids' achievements and encouraged them to believe in themselves. As a young girl she was not very confident, but it was Mrs Malcolm who started to turn this around and make Mandy believe in herself. Before Mrs Malcolm, none of her other teachers had ever really made her think that she was good at anything. It was Mrs Malcolm who first told her that she could write really well, and there would be a particular joy when, arriving in the classroom, she would spot one of her pieces of work on display.

There is one occasion which stands out in Mandy's mind to this day. The class had been tasked with writing a short science fiction story, which had duly been handed in for marking. Whilst Mrs Malcolm was handing back the books, she paused and enthusiastically said to the class, 'You've got to hear Mandy's story. It's superb!' She proceeded to read it out to the class, and they all listened intently as she brought the narrative to life with her manner of reading. To begin with, Mandy felt embarrassed at having the spotlight shone on her, but as the reading unfolded she became increasingly proud and an embryonic thought was born: maybe she was quite good at writing. Without the impact that Mrs Malcolm made in boosting her confidence, it is doubtful

1 A series of exercise-based grammar textbooks.

whether Mandy would have ever pursued her interest in writing. Ms Malcolm's marking was always very detailed, giving both credit and suggested areas for improvement. Mandy still has the science fiction story with Mrs Malcolm's encouragement on it in her 'immaculate handwriting'.

> 'A splendidly planned story. You've set the scene really well, pictured the new society very clearly, and led up to its downfall and the whole point of the story really well.'

One thing led to another and as a teenager she wrote and wrote and wrote. She would stay up late writing stories and by the time she went to university, the die was cast. Her ambition was to be a published author. She had a short story published by Virago and then wrote a script for a television play. Whilst it never made it to the screen, she was pretty chuffed when the script editor told her that she had talent. She continued writing on and off throughout her university years and for a couple more years after that before life got in the way. The twin needs of earning a living and bringing up her daughter meant that writing was put on the back-burner for a while.

However, the spark which had been ignited by Mrs Malcolm never left her and smouldered away. After graduating from the University of St Andrews she went to work as a PA to the vice chancellor at the University of Leicester and then on to the BBC, where she worked on children's radio, from where she progressed to doing a PGCE and then became a highly successful teacher with a career spanning 26 years.

The idea of writing never left her, though. In 2009 she started to write again: first, a comedy set in a Leicester school. This caught the attention of an agent at a prestigious literary agency in London and they requested a copy of the full manuscript. Whilst this did not ultimately lead to a contract, it was a big boost to her confidence and Mandy moved on to writing erotic romance novels. She can only wonder at what Mrs Malcolm would make of that, but success has bred success and she has had seven books published to date. All of this, Mandy believes, would not have been impossible without the input of Mrs Malcolm.

If Mandy met Mrs Malcolm now, she would want to thank her for being the teacher who saw potential in her and encouraged her to believe in herself. Mandy doesn't remember too many of her teachers, but she has never forgotten Mrs Malcolm.

Mandy, just before meeting Mrs Malcolm

Mandy, teacher and author

Mrs Malcolm, c. 1980s

The difference?

Life has been likened to a train journey. We board the train at birth and we share our carriage with an ever-changing cast of people. Some will get off the train and, once departed, we hardly remember them, whilst others leave a deep impact on our lives. It is like this with our teachers. We are guessing that most people will have had 50 or so teachers from the moment they first arrive on the educational stage at the age of 4 or 5 to the moment they launch themselves into adult life. So how come some teachers are so eminently forgettable and we retain special memories of maybe only one or two?

Many a lesson has been derailed because, in the kids' eyes, it is boring. This is the most damning indictment of a lesson or, indeed, a teacher. Time and again when we have spent time with kids who are finding the going tough, they have told us that things are not working out because they find lessons boring. The first base for every teacher in every lesson is to engage the class. Not all subject matter has an immediate appeal. Fronted adverbials and Pythagoras's theorem are not part of kids' day-to-day chat on social media. Even what appears to a teacher to be the most interesting of topics, if wrongly pitched, will become a tedious form of classroom torture for some kids. Let's face it. Kids are not designed to sit still, listen and do as they are told. The teacher's job is to create the desire to learn within them, to make them want to engage in the subject matter and therefore boost their life chances. The very best teachers look for creative and inventive ways of doing this, using all manner of devious devices to 'catch' their classroom prey. From ingenious resources, to play acting and humour, they infect kids with their enthusiasm for the topic.

Mrs Malcolm taught interesting lessons, lessons which engaged and enthused the kids. She read books and stories in a way that engaged her pupils and captured their imaginations. Previous teachers of this class had tried and failed; they had made no impression. Mandy tells us that Mrs Malcolm was incredibly patient with this challenging class and – like all of the incredible teachers in this book – was kind and warm, developing the relationships that helped open the windows of her pupils' minds.

Each teacher will develop their own repertoire of ways of getting the kids involved. This will depend on age and stage, on subject matter and the physical boundaries of the teaching area, and, above all, on that particular teacher. Some teachers are natural extroverts and thrive on big 'boom bang-a-bang' lessons which are experiences in their own right; others are cast in a quieter mould but are equally effective. There isn't a right or a wrong way, as long as you find *your* way that has *that* impact. Put yourself in the shoes of the least well-motivated child in the class and think, 'How can I plan this lesson so that child wants to get involved with the learning?' Assume that they have no interest in the topic at all and build the learning experience from there.

Before we move on, a word about Mrs Malcolm's marking. Let's face it, it's not on anybody's list of reasons for becoming a teacher. 'Oh, I know, I'd love to spend hours and hours marking pupils' work.' It certainly wasn't a top priority for many of the teachers we had in our school days; neither of us can remember much in the way of feedback from our secondary school teachers in the 1970s. The odd 'satisfactory' or 'good' was probably about as detailed as it got, but nothing in the league of Mrs Malcolm, who clearly would be regarded highly in the present climate, in which there is a focus on providing high-quality feedback. This mattered to Mandy at the time and it is interesting that she still has Mrs Malcolm's written words to look back on. She was a teacher ahead of her time.

MAKE YOUR FEEDBACK COUNT

The second vital attribute of Mrs Malcolm was that she made her pupils believe in themselves. Very few of us arrive in school full of the self-belief that we can shine in every area of the curriculum. In fact, the forces of negativity in our minds are much stronger than the forces of positivity, and we say things to ourselves that we wouldn't dare to say to others. We tell ourselves that we are rubbish at maths or that we can't draw. The teachers who get the best out of us are the ones who dig their way into our subconscious, nibbling away at the 'I can't' and substituting it with a 'can do' ethos.

Chris was a cricket enthusiast at school and had a certain disdain for athletics, which he regarded as an intrusion upon cricket in the summer PE curriculum. He never shone at any of the disciplines. One day, after his PE teacher encouraged him, playing on his obvious sporting ego, Chris decided to semi-sprint the 400m, as much for a laugh as anything. Expecting it to go badly wrong at any point, he pushed himself. But it didn't. To his surprise he did pretty well, so much so that the

PE teacher took him to one side and persuaded him that he would be good enough to earn a place in the school team. He started to believe, for the first time, that athletics had something in it for him.

FOCUS YOUR PRAISE ON EFFORT

On a daily basis, search for opportunities to spend that moment with each and every child, making them believe. Do this systemically and regularly. It is easy to think that you are doing it and that you are covering every child, but it is equally easy to overlook some children, often because you are making an earnest effort to engage the more reluctant. The kids who do the right thing day in, day out get less of your time and attention. Work on your praise strategies, building up your repertoire of effort-focused approaches to recognition and reward, and – most importantly of all – know your kids. Mandy felt so proud when she saw her work on display and she enjoyed hearing her story read aloud. But a different child would cringe with embarrassment and retreat into their shell. Every child is different and every child matters. They all need to believe.

Chapter 12

Mr Richardson

Teachers can become that special teacher in a young person's life for a variety of reasons, as we are exploring throughout this book, but sometimes fate seems to declare its hand and teachers find themselves in the right place at the right time. This was the case with Mr Richardson, who was nominated by a recent member of his tutor group, Isla.

Mr Richardson's specialist subject at the secondary school in Lincoln where his path crossed with Isla's is design technology, but it was as a form tutor that he really made a difference. The story did not start all that auspiciously. Mr Richardson took over the form in Year 9 and the students took a while to transfer their loyalty to him from their previous tutor. Isla herself admits to having reservations about him when she learned that he was taking over the form, and there was a fair bit of suspicion on the part of most of the students. Over time, though, he started to win them all over, not least Isla.

She wasn't finding the going especially easy at school. She was not a natural scholar, her dyslexia was making the going pretty tough, and friendships had come and gone over her first few years at the school. She had resigned herself to thinking that she would just get her head down and get through it. She is a strong character with a loyal and supportive family behind her, and she just pressed ahead as she headed for her GCSEs. As relations with Mr Richardson started to thaw, she found in him a kindred spirit.

He made her smile and they developed a great banter. Without drawing attention to the fact that he was making space to support her, he made time for her. Isla summed it up like this:

> 'There are nice people and nasty people, but by being nice you can change someone's outlook.'

There was no magic potion involved. He did the simple things but he did them well: he listened and tried to make her life that little bit easier. They shared jokes and were always ready to have a laugh, which brightened Isla's day.

She reckons that she doesn't know where she would be without him. She had difficulties with getting into school on time. Of course, Mr Richardson could have applied all the usual penalties, but he played it differently. He would create time for Isla to get some breakfast down her before she started the day. He would contrive an opportunity to offer her a cuppa at lunch and break times, which, of course, doubled as an opportunity to catch up and touch base. After school he would make time and space for her to stay behind and complete her work, giving her constant support and encouragement. He went way beyond the call of duty to be there for her and guide her through, because he saw something in her. He knew that she was a good canoeist outside of school, and he was certain that with the right support she could make something of herself in school. The fact that she secured some very respectable GCSE results is testament to what she went on to achieve, and it wouldn't have happened without Mr Richardson's steadying hand.

Suddenly her life at school became bearable and she can't thank him enough for being the teacher who gave her a reason to want to come to school. Without him she doesn't know where she might have ended up. It was during Year 11 that fate was to intervene again when Isla was diagnosed with thyroid cancer. This coincided with the closure of the school to all but a few pupils because of the 2020 coronavirus pandemic, which meant that for many their school days just petered out in isolation at home. You might have imagined that, even without the due rites of passage like the end-of-year prom, that cohort of Year 11s would have been effectively signed off. Not so with Isla.

Throughout all the trauma for both Isla and her family, Mr Richardson was ever present. He was the first port of call for the family. Far from retreating into the distance, he took his place centre stage. One of the challenges that any family has when serious medical challenges arise is determining who needs to know and how much they need to know. No need to worry about that for Isla's family. Mr Richardson took charge. He became the mouthpiece but also the conduit for all the staff to stay in contact with Isla throughout her periods of hospitalisation. She received a steady flow of emails and cards, all masterminded by Mr Richardson. He became the ringmaster, coordinating all communications between Isla and the school. He took the initiative and organised a bag of presents from all the other teachers, but, best of all, he came round for a socially distanced tea party to see Isla at home as she convalesced after her surgery. He made her laugh, he made her smile, he made her feel loved, and Isla would like to thank him a million times over for all the support he gave to her and her family.

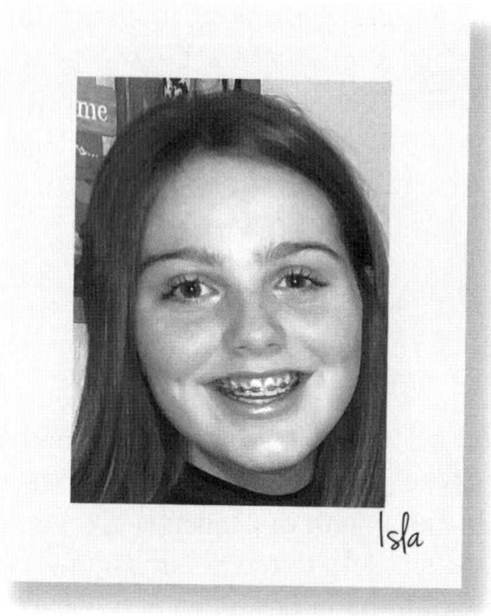

Isla

Mr Richardson

The difference?

It is a joy to be able to celebrate a teacher who made a difference in their capacity as form tutor. It has been our experience that there is a kind of false dichotomy between pastoral and academic roles, particularly in secondary schools. Worse than that, we have sadly encountered teachers who downplayed their pastoral role and would protest at having to deliver a pastoral curriculum, for which they felt ill equipped. Beyond being glorified register takers, they never attached any particular importance to the role and significantly underplayed the impact they could have on the kids in their tutor group. The Craig Richardsons of this world paint a different picture.

GREAT PASTORAL CARE UNDERPINS GREAT LEARNING

The academic curriculum is, of course, very important, but it rests on the foundations of the school's pastoral system. The stronger the foundations, the taller the growth of academic success. And whilst we are holding this hot potato, let's throw the arts and PE into the mix. These are subject areas not to be undervalued and – like the pastoral system – they play a huge role in the school's academic success. For many pupils, such subjects are the areas where they feel at home and are the beacons of light in the trials and tribulations of the bits of the curriculum that they are not naturally drawn to or find tough.

One of the most telling details in Isla's story is that her relationship with Mr Richardson didn't get off to the best of starts. Kids are often very loyal to their teachers, and when a new teacher takes over, they have to win their spurs with the class, who will then give them permission to teach them. At first the respect offered can be grudging at best. This can be particularly noticeable when you move schools. Chris remembers moving from a school where he was a very successful head of year, arriving full of confidence in his new school, only to be rocked by kids who didn't know him being pretty challenging as they pushed the boundaries to see where he was at. It didn't take long before he began to get the key players in his pocket, but he was rather nonplussed to start with. The lesson here is that whenever you start with a new class or in a new school, your reputation counts for nothing. You have to build those positive relationships all over again. Mr Richardson took the time to build his relationship with the form, and once that relationship is built on secure foundations, kids become astonishingly loyal.

LOOK FOR WAYS FORWARD

Another thing we can draw from Isla's story is the way that Mr Richardson approached the problem of Isla's lateness and reluctance to come to school. He could of course have gone down the traditional punishment or penalty route. For sure the school's behaviour policy would have prescribed how this should be dealt with, but Mr Richardson came at the problem from a different angle. He could have punished Isla for her lateness, but would that have made a child who was not very keen on coming to school at the best of times more likely to arrive on time or would it have resulted in, at best, a reluctant compliance, which would soon revert? Or was there another way? Was there a way in which he could get Isla to buy into wanting to do what he wanted her to do?

One of the issues with using punishment as a means of getting pupils to do something is that punishment does not create a love for that thing. We'd really like to be introduced to someone who suddenly developed a passion for Shakespeare after being given detentions for not doing their homework on him. Yes, we know, as you shout at the page, punishments are intended as deterrents. But we see a teacher's role as being proactive and looking to inspire before getting to the deterrent point. For some kids, the code to cracking their safe of engagement might be tricky to find, but it's well worth looking. Even the most disinterested of pupils will have a hook they will bite if offered. And if, as a teacher, you can find it, you will often find that their pals join your 'club' too. Mr Richardson came at the problem from a totally different angle and the result was a young person who became more engaged with school, and who achieved creditable success at the end of Year 11.

So, we are not saying that there is no place for punishments and penalties. There is the *right* place for punishments and penalties. What we are asking is how soon can you become the teacher that never has to use them? We've met quite a few who don't. But – you might retort – what about other kids who were late? Surely, they would be resentful if they felt that Isla was getting preferential treatment? Quite so. That is where the teacher needs to square the circle with them too. Any regime which prescribes a uniform response to a particular problem will fail to cater for those at the margins. The response must fit the child. Our experience has always been that kids will accept differences and nuances of approach, but only as long as they can see the rationale and feel that their point of view has been listened to as well.

Schools are busy places. There is a large concentration of people in confined spaces who are expected to conform to a pretty rigid set of expectations, which have to be established if chaos is not to prevail, but there will always be children who don't fit the mould. Some thrive, some don't. Maybe they don't gel with their peer group, maybe nothing about school life appeals to them, maybe they are looked-after children or, for a multiplicity of other reasons, they don't feel that they fit in. Things were not working out for Isla and school was a daily struggle. Mr Richardson sensed that and his intervention gave her a reason to want to come to school. There are children who naturally slip under the radar, and it is the gift of inspirational teachers to spot them and be there for them, championing their cause and making them believe that school has something for them. Metaphorically speaking, they hold their hand and say, 'It's alright, I am here for you and you will be OK.'

YOU CAN BE A SAFE HAVEN FOR KIDS WHEN THEY NEED ONE

The final hallmark of the role that Mr Richardson played for Isla was that when adversity struck, he stepped up. Young Gary was given a priceless piece of advice early in his career: 'Go out of your way to be kind. After all, you often have no idea about what is going on in that child's life.' Chris reckons that would be a good maxim to take out into the wider world. If only more of our national discourse was based on that principle. All sorts of pitfalls await us in life: children will suffer bereavements, family discord, bullying in and out of school, imprisonment of a family member or even, as in Isla's case, serious health issues. Sometimes these can be latent and kept hidden away by the child, which is where staff – and that means *anyone* who works in a school, not just teaching staff – can play a key role by making sure that their antennae are picking up those signals which make the lights on the dashboard flash. Being that teacher who guided a child through a difficult patch will not just increase their life chances, but also ensure a lifetime's legacy of gratitude, and is maybe just one of the things that elevates teachers to the pantheon of the gods and helps to make teaching the best job in the world.

Chapter 13

Mrs Erwin

Around 600 million years ago your ancestors took a different path to those of other species.[1] Some went on to become leaders in the field of living without bones: jellyfish, sponges, ants and molluscs, for example. However, the rest literally ended up walking a different path and became the vertebrates of this world, eventually evolving into the line of animals that lead to our species, Homo sapiens, and of course, eventually, you.

The difficulty with ancestry, as anyone who has tried to research their family tree will know, is that the further back in time you go, the trickier it gets. Gary has managed to get back to the early 1700s for many lines of his family, but keeps finding that he runs out of leads as the records fade. For the line to be true, you can't guess at it; it must be an accurate family tree. Somewhere back in the mists of time we have ancestors that swam. Others might have roared. Some could have laid eggs. In order for all of us to exist there is an unbroken line of ancestors of all shapes and sizes all the way back to that fork in evolution and beyond.

What is mildly frightening is that if one of your direct animal ancestors was eaten by a dinosaur or another predatory animal, you would not be here.[2] There seems to be a huge element of chance in the very fact that we are here to write this book and you are around to read it. In exactly the same way, it was chance that led a young Mike Bushell to meet a teacher who would, with one persuasive act, change the course of his own personal evolution and pave the way for incredible twists and turns in his life. Like the split in human evolution, the split in Mike's educational direction had an incredibly powerful effect across time (albeit over slightly fewer years, beginning not 600 million years ago, but in 1982).

1 Peter Godfrey-Smith, *Other Minds: The Octopus and the Evolution of Intelligent Life* (London: William Collins, 2018), pp. 40–41.

2 We recommend you read the short story 'A Sound of Thunder' by Ray Bradbury in his anthology of short stories, *The Golden Apples of the Sun* (New York: Doubleday and Company, 1953).

Until he met Pauline Erwin, Mike was first and foremost into sciences. Upon joining secondary school he was intent on pursuing his interest in becoming a zookeeper, having little confidence in any other direction, especially the arts. Mike describes himself as a shy teenager, not at all like the confident presenter we see on TV today, but – unlike many of the stories we have written in this book – the change that happened in Mike was largely due to a single persuasive act on Mrs Erwin's part.

Both of us have a love of accents. We travel the UK presenting in schools and it is a delight to hear the diversity of children's voices. What is also special is how these accents travel, and in schools we find them amongst our youngsters in every corner of the UK – Scousers who've moved to Newcastle and Geordies now living in London. We're not just fascinated with accents from our little island though. We've heard them from much further flung places, from South Africa to China and from Italy to Peru. We are sure that having a teacher with an interesting voice that is a little different to yours and your friends' adds a little something (please note that we are not suggesting you develop a strong regional accent). This was exactly how the teenage Mike saw it and the way in which he describes Mrs Erwin's lilt illustrates it nicely.

> 'She had a beautiful Irish teaching voice, engaging and inspiring.'

Mrs Erwin's engaging manner drew in her pupils as she taught them English and drama. Her patience and motivational manner raised their game as they became drawn into her subjects. Mike remembers that one of the key factors that made her stand out was that she didn't take the typical teacher–pupil approach that he'd experienced before. She made you, the learner, feel part of the creation of the learning: an equal partner in the process. Lessons were not inflicted upon you; you were an integral part of them.

It was this particular approach that made her so persuasive when it came to getting her pupils to do something outside of their comfort zones. For Mike it came when she approached him to take on a main role in a play she was directing: *Hobson's Choice*.[3] Initially, for a shy young Mike this was a terrifying idea and he suggested he would be

3 By Harold Brighouse. E-book available at: http://www.gutenberg.org/files/6347/6347-h/6347-h.htm.

much better off helping behind the scenes. However, he'd not calculated on Mrs Erwin's doggedness and after weeks of nibbling away at him, he relented and agreed to take on the role of Willie Mossop. This was the evolutionary fork in Mike's life and the moment he took a new direction that would lead him to have an extraordinary career and incredible experiences, ironically, like the character he portrayed in *Hobson's Choice*, developing confidence and the courage to take on new challenges.

The play was a great success (although Mike did manage to get stuck in a trapdoor at one point), so much so that on the strength of it Mike changed his A level choices to arts subjects and was offered a place at the National Youth Theatre in London. From there he went on to take a degree in drama at King Alfred's College, Winchester – now the University of Winchester – gradually increasing in confidence and self-belief, and improving his communication skills so much that he joined two bands in the early nineties: Don't Push the River and Arthur the Stoat,[4] moving into acting for a small company and then playing a Roman centurion for Winchester tourism.

In another evolutionary twist, Mike took a job on a local newspaper, followed by a job as a local reporter for the BBC. Then, drawing on his acting skills, he moved into presenting and on to BBC Breakfast, where we often see him trying out all manner of sports as a sports reporter. But possibly the most unusual twist for Mike was when he became a contestant on *Strictly Come Dancing*. Mike tells us that his dance partner Katya Jones – who, of course, became his new teacher – was another incredible motivator, lifting his confidence every week to be able to tackle challenging moves, live on national television in front of a huge audience.

Mike is very clear about who he credits for everything he has achieved and experienced in his career. Without Mrs Erwin seeing something different in him and persuading him to take a leap of faith, Mike would not have had the spark to ignite the flame that continues to spread the exciting fires of Mike's future.

4 We recommend looking up 'Havn't Ya Seen Enuff' by Arthur the Stoat on YouTube. Available at: https://www.youtube.com/watch?v=esgoWr1T-dE.

Mike at secondary school

Mike the TV presenter

Pauline Erwin, present day

The difference?

Maybe there was something in the water in Harrogate[5] in the early 1980s, or maybe it was just fate that Mike Bushell would move to the very secondary school where a patient and kind teacher with a keen eye saw something in him that others hadn't. Who knows? But what we do know is that Pauline Erwin was *that* teacher in Mike's life. The impact of her input has been monumental.

What is particularly interesting in this story is that Mike hasn't told us in detail about Mrs Erwin's teaching methods. In fact, we didn't feel the need to enquire further as the key thing for Mike is really down to one act of brilliance – a trait that so many incredible teachers have: the ability to see something different in their pupils, to dissect their skill set, their talents, interests, abilities and aspirations, and put their finger on *the* thing that will elevate them to a new level. It's not accidental that we have used the word dissect, as the process is almost surgical. There is no best guessing, no thinking, 'I wonder what would happen if I gave Mike a pop at that play.' There is complete clarity and faith that as a teacher they know their pupils in great depth.

STEER THEIR DESTINY

We cannot tell you how important it is for a teacher to build up such knowledge of their pupils. We talk about this in other ways, but in this case, we imagine Mrs Erwin gradually building up her knowledge of her pupils, and in this specific case, Mike. Whatever it was that opened Mrs Erwin's eyes to Mike's potential in the arts we'll never know, but it was a moment of brilliance. In fact, had the *Strictly* judges seen it, they'd be waving the 10-point scorecards with huge enthusiasm.

The additional key aspect of this teaching success story is that Mrs Erwin was like a dog with a bone. Having spotted the key to unlocking Mike's potential, she was not going to let him escape into his comfort zone. When we give presentations to teachers we often talk about using the whole school to build up relationships with those pupils you really need to get in your pocket: popping up everywhere – from the bus queue to the dining room – with smiles and warm words, gradually

5 Pun intended!

developing the relationship. In this case, we imagine Mrs Erwin doing the same but with the goal to gain Mike's trust and persuade him to take the role in the play.

NEVER GIVE UP

In our many years in schools we have been involved with lots of variations of what is now known as 'pupil voice', whereby the kids get involved in the leadership of the school by offering opinions, taking on designated roles and generally becoming more active in the school community. We have learned many things from our involvement with so many incredible young people, but one key thing that teachers tell us that their pupils prefer is teachers who challenge them. You might think that kids want an easy life. 'Give me some colouring in and I'll be happy.' But no. What kids want is to not be stuck with things they find easy; they want to be pushed. Delving further though, we found that it's not good enough just to challenge. The teachers who provide the support to help their pupils raise their game and give them the confidence to take the leap and fly are the ones who are often revered.

Mrs Erwin did all of those things for Mike, having a rapid but lifelong impact. In typical sports reporter style, he sums it up with a wonderful analogy:

> 'It was like Jamie Vardy being in the reserves at Fleetwood Town and a year later playing for England.'

Chapter 14

Mr Hounsome

One of the things we are often asked over coffee during training with a group of NQTs is how we might suggest they manage their work–life balance. We think that this is a trick question, because not everyone has the same in-school pressures or the same lives outside of work. We do pass on many tips to ensure that they are aware of how to manage their workload and how to approach their boss if things build up to pressure cooker level. In addition, we always advise people to ensure that they set aside time for themselves, their families and their interests beyond school. Early in his career, Chris was advised to leave school 'early' one day a week so he had time to do some of these things. We know what it's like, we've been there. We've marked until midnight, written improvement plans into the small hours and spent weeks away from our families on school trips. It's not easy.

The trouble with teaching is that it is more than a job. We both have walked around supermarkets and bought more expensive items as we thought we could use the packaging for a display or a prop in some classroom activity. We've regularly woken up in the night and written down the ideas that came to us in our dreams or whilst snoozing. The 'problem' for both of us was that when it came to work–life balance, teaching was a part of life and, because we enjoyed it, our jobs and our 'lives' became seamless. The issue we would have is if the former overpowered the other to the detriment of our health or other things. We know it's not just teachers who have this way of thinking. It happens in other professions too, but not many. It's much easier if working hours and responsibilities have definite stops and starts, but teaching is not like that.

On one of those school trips we got chatting to our coach driver. We knew him well as he'd taken us to all manner of places over the years. He told us that he loved coach trips himself. He'd been all over Europe as a driver and then again as a passenger. He couldn't get enough of it – a proper busman's holiday.

However, this is the story of Mr Hounsome, a teacher who, for fun, did even more teaching! Trevor Hounsome was a very successful music teacher for many years and retired in 2020. He led the music department for a long time, is well known in music teaching circles and is an examiner of the subject at GCSE level. Like any teacher his week-days were busy. Lessons, duties, reports, parents' evenings ... you know the stuff. You might have heard the popular culture phrase that goes something like, 'He was a mild-mannered reporter by day and a superhero by night.' Well, that was Trevor. A music teacher by day and ... a music teacher by night!

Yes, there was nothing Trevor liked more than to teach more music, and 14-year-old Christopher Small first met him when he joined the brass band of which Trevor was musical director. Christopher had already been playing the euphonium for a few years when he joined. He had good peripatetic teachers at his school and had regularly played in the school orchestra in shows and concerts. However, upon first meeting Trevor he began a new trajectory that would raise his playing to very different heights.

Learning an instrument is difficult. Both of us have tried and failed and are in awe of those who can.[1] Gary remembers a lad he was at school with who was learning the violin. He regularly came home from school, climbed the stairs and passionately practised in his room. At least that's what his parents thought. What in fact was happening was that he was reading comics whilst playing a tape recording of a practice session. This went on for weeks until he was caught out because his mother twigged that he always sounded the same. She sneaked upstairs and burst into his room, finding him with his face in a comic and his tape player blasting out dodgy violin music. Christopher may well have preferred to read comics or play video games than practise his euphonium and tells us that he did feel that practising was a bit of a chore. That is until he met Mr Hounsome.

Suddenly, here was a music teacher who made him *want* to practise. Someone who raised him up by the way he spoke to him, helped him puff out his chest and feel that he could do the difficult things that were being asked of him. So, from chore to challenge, the newly motivated Christopher would gleefully practise, never thinking that this was something imposed on him, but rather a mission to accomplish.

1 In fact, we are green with envy!

Christopher fed from the positivity and enthusiasm he received from his new teacher. He recalls:

> 'He always focused on the positives in my playing and then gave me pointers for improvement. I wanted to repay him and this is why I worked hard on practising.'

You might have already picked up that we do like to have the odd chuckle in our writing. Can you imagine how disappointed we were when we found out that Mr Hounsome's specialist instrument was the cornet and not the trumpet, especially when Christopher told us that his teacher would quite often model what he wanted Christopher to do by blowing his own ... cornet! See, it could have been a good punchline if only he had a trumpet.

Christopher likened his teacher's approach to that of a baker, gradually kneading the bread dough until it reaches exactly the right elasticity. Little by little, with this approach, Christopher's own personal fine-tuning became better and better. Of course, it wasn't all plain sailing. Christopher would mess up. In fact, he remembers when he was first given responsibility for a solo in a competition and he blew it, literally. As he was playing he knew it was all wrong and glanced over to his teacher, who just smiled at him. Mistakes meant opportunities for improvement. Instead of highlighting them as errors, Mr Hounsome stressed that they were things to improve on.

Christopher was inspired to pursue a career in music and started by studying at the Royal Birmingham Conservatoire. During his third year of studies he joined a band in Birmingham which was fortunate enough to be signed to Jools Holland's record label. Things then took off at rapid speed with tours, recordings and gigs. Things with the band came to an end towards the end of his degree, when he was once again inspired by Mr Hounsome. He became a teacher, following the yellow brick road to work with the head of music who he now calls Trevor. Christopher still plays music to a high level outside of his teaching career. He has performed with The Cure, Mumford and Sons, Seasick Steve, The Bluetones, the Welsh National Opera and the Grimethorpe Colliery Band, to mention just a few.

It is obvious when talking to Christopher that working with the man who inspired him so much is magical. He feels that the partnership they have is very special but is sad that it must come to an end. He hopes that he can continue his career in a manner, just like the boy who practised, that will repay everything Trevor Hounsome has done for him.

Chris Small in full band regalia

Mr Small the teacher

Mr Hounsome

The difference?

At the start of this book we mentioned that there are not many professions in which the workers do extra work for little or no pay. You might argue that if a teacher chaperones a school trip abroad during term time, it's within their working week so they are being paid for it, and to some extent you'd be right. The fact is that if that same teacher was back at school, doing their day-to-day job, at the end of the day they wouldn't have a coach load of pupils to look after. Neither would they have to ensure they had breakfast and all their other meals. So, there is some overlap, but without doubt it is beyond the teacher's contract to do these things. However, many do spend their whole careers doing so. Mr Hounsome did those things too, but he also found time every week to do more teaching. It wasn't even that he was doing something different. He was a music teacher, teaching more music. He had a love of music and a love of teaching. So, this was a labour of love for Trevor.

MAKE SURE THE KIDS KNOW YOU LOVE YOUR SUBJECT

But we are not here to discuss the merits of Trevor Hounsome's exceptional commitment to teaching and music; we want to know what he did differently to turn a young Christopher Small from a decent euphonium player, who saw practice as something he had to do rather than a choice he was making, to a person who ate up the learning opportunities Trevor was giving him and built a desire to work hard. This is arguably what teaching is all about. Taking a person and raising their knowledge, understanding and ability to a new level. The step beyond that is taking that person, as a willing participant, to a level they had no idea they could achieve.

What Mr Hounsome did first was give Christopher a different perspective. Mistakes didn't matter; how you dealt with them did. One of the words we don't like to hear in teaching is 'but'. 'That's a really good drawing but ...' 'You've got the right answer but ...' The use of the word 'but' focuses on the negative and, as a learner, this is what you will typically hear first. By simply rephrasing the message, a teacher can make a statement that is much more likely to result in positive gains. 'I really like the way you have used shading in your drawing this time. I can tell you listened to what I was saying and have worked on that. Now, the next step is to …'

The use of praise related to effort and outcome focuses the pupil on what they have done well and how they have done it. The next step is to challenge them in a positive manner. It seems obvious, doesn't it? We challenge you to listen to your colleagues and see how many times they pull the rug out from under their own feedback by dropping a 'but' in. Go a step further, get a colleague to do the same for you. Whether it's spoken feedback or the written word, it makes no difference. Quality feedback links what has been done to the next learning opportunity and is much more likely to be successful if it has a positive emphasis. This is what Christopher identifies as a turning point for him.

The second key thing to highlight here is how Mr Hounsome used his own skill to demonstrate what he wanted Christopher to do. He modelled techniques and style so that it was clear what Christopher was aiming for. Modelling is a key skill of brilliant teachers, whatever the subject or topic. The mere act of demonstrating the route to improved learning often can help pupils really grasp a concept, especially if the process is carefully explained and narrated. Whether it is an English teacher modelling descriptive writing on a whiteboard whilst narrating their thought processes, changing and developing the writing as they go, or a geography specialist walking and talking the process of thinking their way through map reading, modelling is a powerful tool.

MODEL WHAT YOU ARE AIMING FOR

The other advantage that modelling can have is that it allows your pupils to see you as an expert. And this, depending on what you do, can have awe-inspiring results. Mr Hounsome's demonstrations, we imagine, would have illustrated just that to Christopher, who no doubt would have listened to this master of musical accomplishment, thinking, 'I want to be that good.' Gary remembers watching a lesson in which the PE teacher introduced the group to gymnastics by walking into the gymnasium on his hands. The class were spellbound. The teacher told them that they wouldn't be aiming to walk on their hands that day but, with effort, they would all be able to learn a new technique in that session. The group, to a pupil, worked incredibly hard and, indeed, a huge amount of learning took place. Not only that, but Gary heard several clandestine conversations between pupils who stated their intentions to practise handstands that evening. Just as Mr Hounsome made Christopher believe, the PE teacher inspired his class to challenge themselves. Chris was a French teacher in his heyday and had a colleague who was a native speaker. On one occasion, she came into his classroom to ask him something and they conducted the conversation in fluent French in front of the class. One little lad who was not the greatest French student in the history of time looked on open-mouthed and when she had gone out, blurted out, 'I wish I could do that!' For him, it was a moment of change and his engagement increased from then on. Never miss an opportunity to spread that little bit of magic dust in your lessons – even if it is a party trick! If there is something you can do which will wow the kids, don't hold back. Inspiration is the vitamin of aspiration.

Chapter 15

Professor Avendaño

The Amazon rainforest is possibly one of the most amazing places on earth. The brilliant Sir David Attenborough tells us that there is an 'unbelievable diversity of life' existing there.[1] From hundreds of different types of tree to tens of thousands of species of invertebrates, it is teeming with life. Scientists from the world over have flocked there to carry out research. Many have discovered species previously unknown to science and passed on their learning to us, the public, through their documentaries and inspirational films. So, we want you, our readers, to imagine this next paragraph is being narrated by Sir David Attenborough himself as if you were watching one of his magical documentaries.

Cue, Sir David Attenborough:

> *Deep in the great plains of the Amazon basin, east of the Andes, fed by the Amazon, Itaya and Nanay rivers, inaccessible to humans by road, the great metropolis of Iquitos stretches out into the jungle. This is the largest city in the world that is only accessible by river or air, and is home to over 470,000 humans. It was here, in the year 2000, where the 15-year-old Vladimir Mafaldo Grandez met the teacher who was to change his life.*

Look up Iquitos on a map and you will see how remote it is. So, for a young person growing up there, the rest of the world was a distant place. The internet was in its infancy across the world and despite living in the middle of one of the most interesting and important places in the world, Vladimir found it difficult not to feel limited by it. To him, Iquitos was the world and he found it hard to see beyond it. That is, until he met his new secondary school teacher Professor Avendaño.

Vladimir tells us that there was just something about this teacher that was different for him. He stood out from the other teachers he'd had because he gave him a vision of the future, a completely different view of the world and, importantly, a way to help him open it up. Jorge

1 David Attenborough, *The Living Planet* (London: William Collins, 1984), p. 87.

Avendaño was Vladimir's English teacher and, just like many kids the world over, Vladimir thought that learning another language was pretty much a waste of time. All his mates spoke Spanish, his family spoke Spanish, and Iquitos was a world away from the English-speaking world. Why should he bother learning English?

Professor Avendaño provided the answer. Vladimir tells us that whilst he was blessed with loving parents who valued his education, not all of his peers had that; many struggled at home and experienced difficult times. His English teacher saw this and developed a mantra which he constantly illustrated to his pupils. Learning English was a doorway to the world, to be able to communicate and work with people who were from different backgrounds and different countries. But there was much more to his teacher than that. Professor Avendaño understood his pupils, saw the problems they had both in and out of school and made it his role to support them. Vladimir puts it like this:

> 'He taught in a way that was different. He knew our minds and our hearts, and sought to persuade us that through hard work we could achieve things.'

English lessons, according to Vladimir, were about much more than being able to speak and read a new language; they were lessons for life, teeming with advice on how to be the best person you could be. There were constant suggestions and inspirational thoughts about how his pupils could forge positive paths in their lives, and Professor Avendaño's passion and desire to see his pupils do well in life flipped a switch for Vladimir. English became a subject he enjoyed. Instead of seeing his homework as a chore, he did it with relish. In fact, he pushed himself further, studying on his own to increase his abilities in English.

Vladimir looks back on his school days with Professor Avendaño and knows it was his caring approach that changed his life. In particular, he remembers that his teacher had a wider view, one which went beyond the school gates. He saw his pupils as the future of the city, the country and possibly the world. The messages in his lessons often went further, and Vladimir can see that they were intended to show him and his peers that they had a responsibility towards others, to be good people and to help others. They clearly rubbed off on Vladimir, who has the incredible job of being an interpreter and a tour guide in the jungle. But, beyond that, the extra influence of Professor Avendaño can be seen: Vladimir makes a huge difference in the lives of impoverished families, most of whom live in difficult conditions in the Amazon basin. He regularly collects donations and makes trips up the river to deliver food, supplies and toys to these families. He is indeed making the world a better place by helping others, just as his teacher inspired him to do.

A young Vladimir

Vladimir, present day

Professor Avendaño, present day

The difference?

Professor Avendaño's impact on the young Vladimir in faraway Iquitos started with his passion and enthusiasm for his subject: English. How often have we rued the fact that many of the kids we have taught do not seem to step over the threshold of our classrooms with an inbuilt fascination towards the subject matter that we are charged with transferring into their young minds? There does not seem to be an instant appeal in the mysteries of quadratic equations, the meanderings of rivers or irregular verbs in a foreign language. However, a common theme that applies to so many of the incredible teachers we have seen over the years is that they manage to raise the eyes of the class to the sunlit uplands of knowledge by their mastery of their subject and their sheer energy in communicating it.

Chris was reminiscing with a friend from school recently and they recalled their Latin teacher.[2] Neither of them were immediately captivated by the thrills of learning Latin, until they were in Mr Fisher's class. Mr Fisher wrote ghost stories in Latin and delighted in weaving a web of magic around each and every text. His passion was compelling, and so it was with Professor Avendaño. A key ingredient of every great lesson is that the teacher bristles with enthusiasm for what is in store. They greet pupils at the door fizzing with excitement about the learning which is lying in wait for them. They crackle with enthusiasm as the lesson progresses and tell pupils what a great experience they have had at the end. This is even more vital in lessons in which the topic isn't the teacher's favourite. Most teachers will have those topics which they dread slightly. Those are the ones in which you need to put your acting skills into full Oscar mode and deliver a best actor award-winning performance to sell the lesson to the kids.

But wait, there is more. Professor Avendaño had that uncanny knack of lighting the flame for the kids who were perhaps the least likely to engage. It is an old truism that every child really does matter, and that means that we must meet the needs of every child in the class. Some children will respond well to particular approaches or activities, whilst others respond quite differently. As teachers we never fully know what is going on in kids' lives. Sometimes their frustrations with what life is throwing at them might cause them to behave inappropriately or

2 It's an even tougher job if the language isn't actually spoken any more.

switch off, and in the hurly-burly of school life it can be difficult to find time to do anything other than follow the school behaviour policy, which is often skewed heavily in the direction of a penalty.

Professor Avendaño had a huge gift for getting through to the kids who were having difficulties, whatever those issues might be. His key quality was an ability to listen, to try to understand, and to find a way forward without judging. In the eyes of those kids who had perhaps become accustomed to being told off for not doing the right thing, he was legendary. He was always there for them with a seemingly unlimited capacity for patience. The results were stunning. He made a difference for the better, time and again. His advice was heartfelt, sensitive and thoughtful. It was always focused on the needs of the child. He was a pioneer in child-centred education, so different to those teachers who see their role as being simply to impart knowledge and learning, whatever the cost – force-feeding kids with things that they don't see the point of, don't think they are very good at and don't want to engage with.

IT'S ALL ABOUT THE CHILD

He never lost sight of the big picture. We have spent a lot of time reflecting on and researching the different learning styles of boys and girls. One of the features of successful teaching which comes up over and over again, with boys particularly, is the absolute necessity of presenting the big picture so that kids can see what they are learning now and how it fits into that big picture. As with all these findings we reckon it is not just boys who benefit from such an approach. Once kids get why they are learning something, they are much more likely to engage and benefit from the lesson. Professor Avendaño had a passion for English because he saw it as a way of opening the windows of the mind and the doors of opportunity for his students. The sky was the limit. Much as they were growing up in a large city in a very remote location in Peru, he wasn't content for them to feel limited to a future there. He wasn't prepared to accept that young people from the locality should just accept their lot. He wanted them not just to be citizens of the world but to have a hand in shaping that world for the better. Great teachers inspire their kids with a vision of what they can achieve. They are not content to sit back and leave the privileges of this world for others. They believe in their kids, they rate them as being as good as any, and probably better, and they ceaselessly seek to inspire them to be the very best version of themselves that they can be.

GIVE THEM A VISION

We are sure that Professor Avendaño would be proud of how life has turned out for young Vladimir Grandez. After all, the work goes on. Vladimir is making a difference in the lives of others. You never know where your influence will end.

Chapter 16

Mr Harvey

Unless you have been living in an off-grid bothy in a remote valley on an uninhabited Scottish island, you will have noticed that in 2020 things were far from 'normal', whatever normal is. Life was very different for most people and extraordinarily different for some. The pandemic did bring out the best in so many people, if you ignore a small minority. People worked harder than they had ever done before, saving lives, supporting people and helping others. Teachers had to step up and we found ourselves in awe as they set and marked work from home, taught in school and, in many cases, taught their own kids at home too. We saw teachers run ragged keeping up with the daily changes in rules and requirements. Never has there been so much pressure on our systems and practices in so many different ways.

Amongst all of this turmoil and tribulation, there have been beacons of light. People who, until this year, were relatively unknown and went about their daily lives without causing much of a ripple beyond their friends and family. Captain Tom, who became a knight of the realm and raised millions for the NHS as he reached his one hundredth birthday by walking lengths of his garden, Leona Harris,[1] a nurse from Bury who raised over £70,000 to buy iPads to help COVID-19 patients connect with their families, and Zane Powles,[2] a deputy head teacher from Grimsby who walked over 550 miles to deliver around 7,500 free school meals to families, are just three of the many.

But there are other ways to bring joy and the internet has been rattling with amazing videos of people who have cheered the nation. From bands who have appeared outside people's houses for impromptu concerts to the Thursday night applause for our NHS staff. You quite simply never know when, or if, your 'fifteen minutes of fame', as Andy

1 Joe Harrigan, Leona Harris: Rossendale-born nurse to feature on ITV advent calender and new Dan Walker book, *Lancashire Telegraph* (20 November 2020). Available at: https://www.lancashiretelegraph.co.uk/news/18885536.leona-harris-rossendale-born-nurse-feature-itv-advent-calender-new-dan-walker-book/.

2 Jenn Selby, Teacher walks hundreds of miles to hand-deliver 7,500 school meals to his hungry students, *iNews* (18 July 2020). Available at: https://inews.co.uk/news/teacher-walks-deliver-free-school-meals-grimsby-556960.

Warhol allegedly put it, might appear.[3] Neither Alix Lewer or Dominic Glynn, as teenagers in the late 1980s and mid 1970s respectively, would have imagined that their music teacher would become a national celebrity in the year 2020. You just wouldn't, would you? But, for both, to see Mr Harvey pop up on a viral YouTube video and then repeatedly on the BBC Breakfast show, it awoke more than a few memories.

Alix and Dominic attended the same school, but at different times. To have two views of the same teacher spanning around 15 years has been wonderful because not only have their stories illustrated that Paul Harvey was a fantastic teacher, but that two teenagers set well apart in school years had so similar a view of their music teacher.

We have interviewed hundreds of teachers for jobs and when we ask what sort of teacher they would be for us, we quite often received similar answers along the lines of, 'I would show my passion for my subject.' But what does this actually mean? What does it look like? Anyone can say it in a letter of application or an interview. But how do you make that passion work for your pupils? Paul Harvey did exactly that and it's quite clear from what Alix and Dominic have told us that he opened up music to every child and engaged with his classes in such a way that the pupils became part of the lesson. Bear in mind, this was pre-national curriculum and pre-Ofsted times. So, there was no national focus on different pedagogies or classroom engagement strategies. This was pure, unrefined Paul Harvey, who would put records on for Dominic's class and ask the kids to express their views. Alix explains that pupils who struggled academically in other areas were supported to be key players within classroom projects and their contributions were taken seriously and valued equally. As Alix says, Mr Harvey:

> 'seemed able to find each student's personal connection with music and use it to help build a bridge to learning and to enjoying the subject.'

3 Rachel Nuwer, Andy Warhol probably never said his celebrated 'fifteen minutes of fame' line, *Smithsonian Magazine* (8 April 2014). Available at: https://www.smithsonianmag.com/smart-news/andy-warhol-probably-never-said-his-celebrated-fame-line-180950456/.

Dominic adds:

> 'He never made me feel inadequate for attempting to make music without the technical know-how of a traditional music training.'

It's no secret that we see the arts as a core subject in schools, one often underestimated by the politicians and civil servants who make educational policy and decide funding directions, but Paul's inclusive approach opened doors for all pupils and had a profound effect on Alix, whose career has developed in a manner which strongly reflects those principles.

> 'Everyone was seen as having the potential to learn, engage and improve.'

This ethos – of everyone being valued – generated trust and mutual respect. We wonder how many pupils of the 2020s are given the keys to the school. Dominic remembers that he and his friends wanted to impress Mr Harvey with their compositions and were rewarded with the keys to the music room, with the words, 'Here are the keys, lads. Give them back to Mr Bullen [the caretaker] whenever you're done.'[4] We cannot imagine this happening now, but quite clearly it gave the young Dominic an extra boost and he and his mates would often use the facility long into the evening.

> 'Without those words, I am certain I wouldn't be able to call myself a professional composer today.'

Similarly, Alix reflects on the approach of her teacher as being a major help in developing her self-confidence. At the time, she was being comprehensively bullied, and must have been more than concerned when she was asked to play a clarinet solo in assembly, in front of her antagonists. Supported by Paul, she pulled it off and strangely had no reprisals from the name-callers who followed her home regularly. She put this down to Mr Harvey's involvement in the assembly and the

4 In fact, Nigel Boyd, who nominated Mr Hope, happened to mention that he also had PE teachers who gave him and his friends a key to the sports hall so they could play football when they wanted to.

credibility given to what she was doing. There were strong expectations in music lessons that there was mutual respect and that spilled over into the corridors and beyond.

'What's the matter with you, Mr Glynn? Are you trying to lay an egg?'

In teacher training we both remember being explicitly told that we should never be sarcastic to our pupils. According to trainees we have worked with recently, this is still a mantra. However, it's not that straightforward. If the relationship you have with a student is positive and well established, if you share a sense of humour and unconditional mutual respect, then we see no reason why you cannot engage in such daftness. Only you can be the judge of the relationship, so tread carefully. There is, however, nothing like a good laugh with your class to help build your relationship with them as a group and as individuals. And let's look at it another way, learning to laugh together – at and with each other – is a key social skill. We guess that Mr Harvey knew that Dominic would not take offence.

Mr Harvey had a great sense of humour and loved to laugh, which Alix describes as a 'booming belly laugh', and this was reflected in his lessons. The creation of fun in lessons is crucial at every age and stage. We often remind trainees that sixth formers love to laugh as much as 4-year-olds, just about different stuff. And, of course, returning to the sarcasm conversation for a second, we're not suggesting that you try this with your Year 1s! Kids love to laugh and it's a key part of creating boomerang kids – you know, the ones who love to come back, the ones who run up to you in the school yard saying, 'Have we got you next lesson, Miss?' You know they know, and they know you know, but they are just excited to be coming back to you again, because learning is fun in your lesson and you have created that positive relationship that makes them feel valued and cared for.

'Mr Harvey's Ford Capri wheel-spinning out of the school car-park is an everlasting memory, as is his booming belly laugh.'

Both Alix and Dominic, like others Paul taught, have been inspired by him to pursue careers in music. Alix, having studied music at the University of Oxford joined the English National Opera's Education and

Outreach Programme, and loved seeing potential realised in otherwise marginalised groups. The core principles of inclusion that she witnessed in Mr Harvey's lessons, and the courage and confidence he gave her, took her via a roundabout route to work in the homeless sector, special education, then speech and language therapy and safeguarding, before establishing the Include Project, a charity which uses music, inclusive communication and laughter to teach us how to include people with understanding and speaking difficulties.[5]

Inspired by Mr Harvey, Dominic was determined to make a career out of music, and after submitting demo tapes to the BBC was lucky enough to be offered the job of composing music for *Doctor Who*. He ended up writing for 15 episodes of the show in the late 1980s and was one of the few composers to be given the prestigious job of rearranging the famous theme tune, originally composed by Ron Grainer. Since then he has worked continuously as a composer and producer of music for TV, film, radio and advertising, as well as producing house and techno music tracks, DJing and running his own record label.

Back to Mr Harvey, who now cruelly has dementia, but is now 'Paul' to both Alix and Dominic, who appeared with him on one of the BBC Breakfast interviews after Paul became a viral internet hit and then a successful artist in the charts. Paul was not only a brilliant teacher, he was also a concert pianist and a fantastic musician. On the viral video, Paul's son, Nick, challenges him to improvise a piece of music based on four notes. He does so with amazing results.[6] The BBC Philharmonic orchestra then picked it up, turned it into a collaborative orchestral piece and released it into the wild. It's stunning. Take a look at the video for yourself and you'll see Paul, witness his passion for music and hear the laugh that was famous amongst his pupils.

5 See www.include.org.

6 See https://www.youtube.com/watch?v=wUGoWKy4HyE.

Alix at school

Alix, present day

Dominic during his sixth form days

Dominic, present day

Paul Harvey, 2020, around the 'four notes' time

The difference?

Back to our introduction and Gary's first day in secondary school. At the age of 11, fully kitted out in his new uniform, he set off for class. At the entrance, prefects – all sixth formers – were observing the arrival of the new kids. They all seemed so tall. The girls looked like women and the lads, well, oddly, they looked like men. He was stunned. Never mind a new school, this was a different planet! It didn't stop there. The school was a huge, confusing maze of a building, the teachers distant and the lessons … well, there was a lot of shouting, and not always by the teachers. On top of this, there were subjects he'd never done before, like French, Latin (very useful in a coal-mining village) and music. All of these subjects were taught from textbooks. Gary cannot remember a single teacher saying, 'Now, turn to your partner and tell them …' or 'Listen to this song and think about how it makes you feel.'

SHOW OFF YOUR SKILLS AND PARTY TRICKS

It would have been so good to have been taught music by Paul Harvey. Maybe Gary wouldn't have two guitars in the loft instead of in his lounge if he had. There is a latent curiosity in kids about their teachers as to whether they are actually any good at the subject they are teaching. They probably wouldn't articulate this in so many words, but they never fail to be impressed by the PE teachers who demonstrate handstands, languages teachers who fall into fluent Spanish, maths teachers who can demonstrate great mental arithmetic skills or music teachers who can really play. Paul Harvey was one of those who would play his piano in lessons, which was mesmerising for his students and helped to engage even the most reluctant in the magic of his lessons. It is worth every teacher coming up with whatever their particular party trick is that will wow the kids. Paul Harvey knew just how to do it and how to make it work for him.

Paul Harvey's lessons were for all kids. He crafted them to engage and invited them to contribute. Both Alix and Dominic would point out that whilst Paul was relaxed and fostered a positive ethos in his lessons, he didn't tolerate poor behaviour. He set high standards and expected his pupils to follow suit. Now that's easy to say, but hard to do. So, what was the superpower that he wielded?

It was the fact that all who entered his class were valued. Whether they were into music, or into a type of music, or not fussed about music, they were all welcome. And his mission was to create learning opportunities to inspire all. It would be unlikely if he inspired everyone – that achievement is not something we've ever come across – but what is quite clear is that his teaching was designed to provide access to music for everyone, and that no matter how inexperienced or opinionated they were, their voices all mattered.

INCLUSION IS FUNDAMENTAL

As Alix points out, when kids turned up with low expectations for their performance in the subject, he wasn't fazed. Paul actively encouraged collaboration and peer support. He challenged his pupils to raise their game, encouraging Dominic's fledgling band and Alix's developing clarinet performances. Like all top-notch music teachers he put on shows and concerts, but – going one step further – he would write the shows and compose the score, often collaborating with others. Alix particularly remembers the joy and nerves of playing in her first stage musical, 'Arf 'n' Arf', written by Paul and Pete Talman, another teacher at the school.[7]

Paul's enthusiasm, creativity and passion for engaging all has changed lives, long before the notion of inclusion became fashionable. Even now, that same passion, albeit on a different stage and at a different age, is still making a difference. And once you make that difference, you never unmake that difference.

7 In fact, Alix seems to have had luck on her side, as she also mentions that after being taught by Paul, she had another teacher who she describes as being hugely influential on her career: Simon Austin, who taught her during her GCSEs and A levels.

Chapter 17

Mrs Baxendale

Are people, in the immortal words of Bruce Springsteen, 'born to run'?[1] Are we born pre-programmed to play a particular role in the world? Was Neil Armstrong born to be an astronaut and the first human being to set foot on the moon? Did the midwife pluck the newborn Barack Obama from the womb and then place him gently in his mother's arms saying, 'He looks destined for the White House'? Did Stephen Hawking pop into the world champing at the bit to decipher the universe?

We're not sure that there is a definitive answer to this, though we have certainly met a few people who – whether it was by destiny, fate or design – have ended up being incredible role models. But it's not all plain sailing. One of Winston Churchill's teachers wrote in his school report that, Winston 'has no ambition'.[2] John Lennon was described by one of his teachers as, 'certainly on the road to failure …'[3] And the middle school head teacher of a young Nick Butter said that he was 'not a natural runner'. We'll let you, our readers, be the judge of that as you read on, but we think that it's important to note here that actually Nick agrees with what his head teacher, David Benson, said and also goes on to say that Mr Benson was an incredibly supportive teacher in his life.

However, we are turning the clock back even further for the beginning of this story. In fact, right back to the very first day a 5-year-old Nick Butter set foot in school as a cripplingly shy lad terrified of the world at large and in particular the social discourse that is associated with it. Later to be diagnosed with dyslexia, Nick arrived at school unprepared

1 Bruce Springsteen, *Born to Run* [album] (Columbia Records, 1975).

2 Quoted in Churchill Centre and Churchill Museum, *Finest Hour: The Journal of Winston Churchill*, 143 (Summer 2009), p. 12. Available at: https://winstonchurchill.org/wp-content/uploads/2017/03/Finest_Hour_143.pdf.

3 Quoted in Valerie Strauss, John Lennon's report card at 15: 'He has too many of the wrong ambitions', *The Washington Post* (9 October 2020). Available at: https://www.washingtonpost.com/education/2020/10/09/john-lennons-report-card-15-he-has-too-many-wrong-ambitions/.

to socialise. Merely talking with other kids was out of the question, let alone collaborating on classroom tasks or even playing a game in the school yard.

Nick needed someone to help him change this and his very first teacher, Mrs Baxendale, was just that person. From the very start she held his hand – literally – as he ventured into the playground, nurturing him and supporting his tentative steps into this new world he'd joined. Gradually, she helped build his confidence, and helped Nick to begin learning how to play with others, and eventually to do so without her company. It wasn't easy, but Mrs Baxendale saw the struggle Nick was having and kept at it, seeing the potential in this little boy and aiming to help him unlock it.

This continued in the classroom and beyond the school day with extra lessons. Nick remembers being shown how to hold a pencil, and how challenging it was to learn how to read, spell and write, describing his as 'extreme dyslexia'. Lessons carried on twice a week after school at Mrs Baxendale's home after a request for her help by Nick's parents. Step by small step, Mrs Baxendale was there through his infant and primary school years, still holding his hand in one way or another. Nick tells us that even though his parents offered some form of financial recompense, it was small compared to the numerous hours and unrelenting patience she had when supporting him. It was slow going, but as far as the developing Nick was concerned, it was OK to fail, because Mrs Baxendale had instilled that into him. Trying and keeping on trying was the key to success and if you failed, that was just part of learning.

Nick loved sport, but team sports were out of the question. In fact, initially, without Mrs Baxendale, Nick wouldn't have contemplated doing any kind of individual sport.

> 'She held my hand as we ran the egg and spoon race on sports day.'

It's hard to imagine that young lad now. From the egg and spoon race aged 5 to his first marathon aged 11. Yes, you read that correctly, 11! Nick lived to run and did very well at it, despite not being 'a natural'. But the lessons he'd learned from Mrs Baxendale about resilience and effort were the magic in Nick's winning formula. At the age of 19 he ran his first competitive marathon and in the same year became part of the British U19 national ski team, before eventually settling on running as his primary sporting focus.

And this is where we show you that Mrs Baxendale's impact has really gone the distance. Nick has now run over 800 marathons (yes, 800 marathons), he's run 100 miles in less than 21 hours, 138 miles in 24 hours, 221 in 48 hours and has on one occasion ran 351 miles. Amazing! Now take a deep breath and read on.

On 10 November 2019 Nick broke four world records and set a further two by becoming the first and only person to run a marathon in every country on the planet. One marathon in each of the 196 countries in the world. That's two or three marathons a week, every week for 96 weeks. He was the first to achieve this incredible physical and mental task, not to mention overcome the logistical and financial complications.

When we spoke to Nick in November 2020, you might have thought there'd be plenty of excuses for him to put his feet up. After all, we were in the middle of a pandemic. You'd be wrong to think that though. We chatted on the phone as Nick ran around Naples with around ten miles to go until he finished yet another marathon for his latest challenge: to run 2,620 miles weaving from the very north to the south of Italy in 100 days. During this challenge Nick's book *Running the World*, the amazing story of his adventure, was published.[4] What is really poignant, though, is how Nick described the challenge of learning to read and write as being equally difficult to running a marathon in every country in the world. He details how Mrs Baxendale's support helped him to make great leaps forward to the point where he is now a bestselling author. The mind boggles considering what he might take on next.

When not running, Nick is a successful international speaker. He even managed to speak in schools as he was running the world, aiming to inspire audiences of any age.

> *Today is a privilege, tomorrow is not a guarantee – what are you waiting for?*[5]

4 Nick Butter, *Running the World: My World Record Adventure to Run a Marathon in Every Country on Earth* (London: Transworld, 2020).

5 See https://www.nickbutter.com/about.

From the lad who wouldn't speak, to a man who speaks to thousands without fear or nerves. He's already had an incredible journey, but we know two things: Nick will find more challenges to tackle and, whether running or not, Mrs Baxendale's legacy is leaping a generation and helping to create the difference Nick is making to the world.

Nick remains in touch with Jenny Baxendale. He still visits her house, but not to write or to study maths, now he sits at the same table with a cup of tea, enjoying the company of the teacher – now a friend – who changed his life.

Nick Butter, having run a marathon in every country of the world

Mrs Baxendale with the young Nick

The difference?

It's difficult to picture the gulf between the Nick Butter of his childhood and the Nick Butter we spoke to whilst he was weaving his way towards the towering Mount Vesuvius. But just like the dormant giant that lay ahead of him on that run, Nick was a dormant giant as he began his first day in school. Whilst we hope that Vesuvius never again unleashes the power it spewed at the world back in 79AD when it destroyed Pompeii and Herculaneum, every teacher hopes that they can release the latent talents and abilities in every child. Jenny Baxendale awoke the sleeping giant in Nick.

What she did sounds simple, but it is anything but that. It's clear that she spotted the potential in Nick from the very outset and set out to do everything in her power as a teacher to help him realise it, to help him see, in his words, that 'the world is there to be had, that opportunities were there for the taking.' Little did she know that she would set such a determined spirit free to achieve such incredible things.

There is no one size fits all in teaching. Teachers like Jenny know their pupils well, take time to establish a positive relationship with them, and – using the knowledge and trust gained – patiently and empathetically begin steering them forward. Jenny didn't force Nick to play with other pupils; she taught him how to engage with them. The steps were small and her patience and care huge, but little by little Nick's world expanded and his confidence grew as she created opportunities for him to take.

When you begin your journey into teaching, one of the fundamental decisions to be made is about the sort of teacher you want to be. Are you going to be like Tarzan? King of your classroom jungle, one yodel and the kids will instantly rally. Or a Moses type figure, leading your pupils to the heady heights of new learning? You could, of course, adopt an authoritarian approach, branding yourself as a stickler for the rules and regulations as laid down by the school's policies. Then again, you could be an upbeat motivator, challenging the kids to be the best that they can be and rallying them to constantly raise their game. We could go on with these stereotypes.

Actually, you need to be all things to all pupils. The very best teachers have all of these approaches in their locker and many more besides. The key is knowing how to pitch it for your class and the individuals within it. Given that you are in the 'changing lives' business, pitching it well is imperative – and the way to nail that is by knowing both the individuals and the group dynamics. You'll need to know when to be strict, when to lead and when to allow the kids freedom. Learning the individual needs, likes, lives and personalities of each pupil in your class is crucial. Some kids will be super confident and not need you steering them constantly; others – like Nick – will need a different approach.

In our favourite educational quote, Haim Ginott points out that teachers are 'the decisive element in the classroom' and that they 'make the weather'.[6] Like a typical forecast chart of the UK, however, the weather needs to be different across the landscape of seats in your classroom. On any one day, you may need to create sunshine to cheer up Haroon, who you have deliberately sat with upbeat Olivia, as he has had a bit of a hard time at home. At the same time, near the front, you need the trade winds to blow on Josh, as he's slow getting going. And Luna, well, she needs some blue skies to help her believe in herself.

The 'weather' you create may well be changeable for every child individually, but you need almost consistent summer warmth in your classroom. Jenny directed the jet stream directly at Nick. He describes her as having 'huge amounts of energy and enthusiasm', generating positive weather to create trust and build the relationship which would enable him to begin to take steps in learning. He needed to feel that she understood him, cared for him and would support him no matter what. In our experience, all kids need this in different amounts and in different doses at different times – which is why it is crucial that you learn and understand how to be the decisive element for each of them.

Jenny Baxendale's weather god status is firmly established.

6 Haim Ginott, *Teacher and Child: A Book for Parents and Teachers* (New York: Macmillan, 1972), p. 15.

Chapter 18

Jason Wood

'If you don't know where you're going

Any road will take you there.'

George Harrison[1]

Both of us started school at the age of 5 and left when we were in our late fifties (as teachers rather than students)! As we forged our careers as teachers, we spent, if you include university, around 50 years each in schools. The road we followed was a pretty simple one, only diverging when we moved schools or roles. But on the road of life, those changes barely cause a swerve. It was easy navigation for both of us. We both knew that teaching was the career we wanted. Chris, from a very early age began teaching his teddies. Each of his cuddlies had an exercise book which he would collect from them and, in red biro, mark their work. He even gave them grades: 9/10. And comments: 'Good try.' And you know from the introduction how we were both inspired by our teachers to become teachers ourselves.

This early desire to teach has made our lives easier in many respects, though some might argue that we have missed out in other ways by not diverging down different paths along our journey. But both of us feel we were destined to teach and would not change any part of our trip at all. There will be lots of people out there in different career roles who have harboured burning desires to become what they are now: footballers, scientists, police officers, nurses, and so on. But for some, life's road is, to quote another song lyric, a 'long and winding road'.[2] The road can be bumpy: full of twists and turns and potholes. This was the road that Jay Boucher took.

It's fair to say that Jay didn't have the easiest start on his journey and his road was full of those gnarly bits that grab and shake you. Jay grew up on a tough estate on the edge of the city, as a mixed-race lad with

1 From the song 'Any Road' (Dark Horse Records, 2003).
2 The Beatles, 'The Long and Winding Road' from the album *Let It Be* (Apple, 1970).

four sisters in a single parent family. Life wasn't easy. Jay tells us he survived the bullying and racism he faced through his interest and ability in sport.

> 'Not to say I got away from it, it just helped me escape it.'

He was a bright lad and arrived at his secondary school with high hopes, but by the time he did his exams, things had changed, especially regarding his motivation, and he left with no GCSE passes. Looking back, he feels there were a number of factors that contributed to this: there was a culture of no challenge and low expectations in his school and the teaching he describes as 'not great'. There was little educational support at home as his mum had had little schooling and struggled with reading and writing. His sisters were developing busy lives of their own. But Jay also takes ownership and points out that, ultimately, he made some bad decisions and rather than step up when the going got tough, he downed tools and refused to ask for help.

Following his GCSEs, Jay went to college with the idea that he'd retake the exams he needed and start studying some new subjects that he'd not yet had the chance to do – like photography. Being brutally honest, he points out that his mindset hadn't changed.

> 'If I'm being honest it was just buying time before I had to get a job. I left college failing everything but if there was a GCSE on drinking, I would have passed that.'

Following that came a series of supermarket jobs over ten years. Towards the end of that time he was chatting with his partner's mum, who mentioned that a friend of hers was a youth worker and that he might do well in that field. He volunteered with his local council and found himself working at the supermarket by day and doing youth work by night, eventually being offered a paid part-time position by the council and the opportunity to do a level 3 NVQ.

At this point a little confidence arrived and, having passed the NVQ, Jay applied for a place at university. With next to no qualifications this was a challenge, but he passed the assessment and did well on the interview. So much so that two universities offered him a place to study on their BA honours youth and community work course.

Both of us remember visiting universities with our own children, checking out the various campuses, resources and courses. It's a big decision and we remember the pressure of making the right decision. For Jay, the choice was easy – after he met Jason Wood. Sometimes it takes something a bit different to change your life, and Jason Wood was different to any teacher or lecturer Jay had ever met. You might be fooled into thinking that it was because Jason had given a brilliantly engaging presentation from behind a lectern. But you'd be wrong.

> 'At the university open day, he stood out instantly because he wore no shoes! And was clambering around opening windows.'

Whilst others talked simply about course content and life on campus, Jason had a different approach, discussing the merits of *Doctor Who* and The Human League.[3] He was different – and for Jay, who was intimidated by this place of higher education (given that he'd failed so much earlier on in his school life), it put him at ease and his decision was made.

For Jay, Jason was simply everything he thought didn't exist in the higher levels of academia. He describes him as having charisma and character and, importantly, for the first time, here was a teacher who made him feel different.

> 'He made me feel welcome.'

Here was a teacher who Jay describes as having an intense method of delivery that engaged him, making him want to learn and helping him retain the information being taught. For the very first time he found himself enjoying education, learning with ease and feeling at home in the classroom.

> 'I had never experienced that prior to his teaching.'

Jay tells us that Jason would teach in an overdramatic style, almost giving the impression that he was crazy, but, at a turn, would bring the room back with something that was calculated and enlightening.

3 For younger readers, a late 1970s and early 1980s pop band.

He would mix youth work with talk about sharks and laser beams, somehow linking that back to the theory and the key learning points. It was total engagement for Jay and he often reflected on the twists and turns of the classroom journey, but it was the content woven into the narrative that was important. This made an indelible imprint on Jay's mind and helped him hugely with essays, assessments and exams. Furthermore, Jay explains that Jason taught him to question and explore things from multiple perspectives, which helped him to think more critically. All of this was achieved through the manner in which he framed questions and the points he made whilst teaching.

This was a three-year degree and Jason moved to another university at the end of Jay's first year. However, the change had occurred. Jason had kindled the fire and set the flames leaping in Jay's learning, making a difference that could never be undone. There was no looking back and the enjoyment of learning and confidence that Jason had ignited in Jay leapt forward.

A successful career in youth work followed, with Jay eventually managing a strand of the local Connexions programme – the system that took over from the careers advice service. But trouble was brewing. The role became more and more politically governed and Jay felt that he was shackled by local politics. The realisation that his role was linked to European funding was the catalyst for change and the winding of the road continued for Jay. But as he says, he could not have taken this new leap without the influence and support of Jason.

In 2018 Jay started his own business, a micro pub, which has won several awards and will hopefully continue to thrive post-pandemic.[4] Jay is quite clear that Jason changed his life and gave him the confidence and drive to become the person he is now. Jason didn't teach Jay how to set up a successful business, how to create a micro pub out of an old general store or how to network with brewers across the UK, but, without a doubt, he helped him navigate his way down the road to it.

> 'I needed motivation, fun and someone to say, "Yes, Jay, you are good enough to be here." Jason gave me that, and I'm so grateful he did.'

4 See www.millhillcaskandcoffee.com.

Jay and his wife, Georgie, at his graduation

Jason Wood, present day

The difference?

The typical expectation these days is that you go to school, gain qualifications, then head off into the big wild world of work or further training. That works for an awful lot of people, but not everyone and certainly not Jay Boucher. What a world it would be if everyone's lives were that simple and ran that smoothly. For Jay, it took 27 years before he found his way onto the right road. It took him 27 years to meet *that* teacher who would change his life.

The good news is that there is always the possibility that something will happen to change someone's direction for the better. It can be the case, as it was for Jay, that life can turn on a pinhead. The impression that Jason made on Jay was immediate. He went from wavering between two universities to knowing with complete assurance which one was right for him. We have heard it said that you can change a child's life with one word, with one moment in time. Maybe something as easy as a smile, a willingness to listen and to show a child that you believe in them. Never, ever give up on a child. When you do find the golden key that opens the way forward, it is the best feeling in the best job in the world. Jay, of course, had to do something to get to Jason, and by taking a leap forward and volunteering in youth work, he set the wheels turning to eventually lead him there. He created his own luck.

MAKE LEARNING FUN AND EXCITING

Jason's teaching style clearly lights up a room. You could be forgiven for thinking that a teacher who leaps about barefoot in the classroom is slightly bonkers. You may, in fact, be right, but we doubt it very much. Jason was even cleverer than that. He broadcast on the students' wavelength to make his teaching memorable. He created a fantastical world around the pop music and television of the day to engage his students, honing his lessons so that he could focus in on the learning. Planning lessons is a craft, involving detailed preparation for each and every stage to make learning happen with constant adjustment and refinement. Time spent planning is never wasted.

Teaching is a role played out before an ever-changing audience. The characters you play are entirely of your own creation. Just as stand-up comedians can often adopt a persona on stage that is entirely different to their real-life one, teachers can do the same. We know many teachers who have created an alternative image of themselves in school: a classroom diva, a dapper dressed role model, a hip musician, a mad professor, for example. But outside of school they are different people, with different behaviours, hobbies and interests.

'All the world's a stage'

William Shakespeare[5]

Indeed, every classroom is a stage. And teachers like Jason play out their Oscar-worthy performances on them. But there is a significant point we need to make here. We've come across teachers who use their stage because they want to perform. They enjoy the gratification from their audience's reaction and, sadly, often forget that their performance is meant to result in great learning. Gary remembers watching a teacher deliver a real crowd-pleasing lesson. The teacher performed to the class for forty minutes, holding them spellbound. Gary remembers laughing out loud himself. However, there was a problem. There was no learning. As good as the performance was, it was a poor lesson because it didn't deliver learning.

USE YOUR SKILLS AND TRAITS TO BE DIFFERENT

Jay, however, points out that Jason always had his eyes on the prize. His performances always held the narrative closely to the learning, which twisted back to the key points and sharply focused on the theories being presented. Jason's acting skills combined with his focus on learning. Knowing when to be on show and when to focus the group on a cleverly worded question is the prize. He was the first teacher to engage Jay, to make his lessons fun and also to give detailed and considered feedback which enabled Jay to take the next steps in his learning. His feedback wasn't just the platitudes Jay had heard before. It was tailored specially to Jay with words that really resonated. If your class are engaged by you as a teacher, having fun, enjoying the lesson whilst you subtly embed the learning in the process, the difference between having fun and learning will be seamless.

The challenge here is to find the right persona for you. We can't all be flamboyant classroom practitioners, but we can all put on our own charisma. This is something you can't be given in teacher training. It's not like you can skip down to your local supermarket and buy charisma in soluble tablet form. It's not something you'll find on Amazon either. But, let's face it, you don't become a teacher because you're a shy and

5 From *As You Like It*, Act II, Scene VII.

retiring introvert. Every teacher has personality and imagination. How you choose to develop that to meet your needs and fit your context is entirely up to you. However, having something that makes you stand out, being Mr or Mrs Different in your classroom, really helps. It made Jason Wood *that* teacher for Jay.

> 'For someone who, in terms of time, I had such a short engagement with, he had such a huge impact in my learning journey. Which is why I consider him my learning hero.'

Chapter 19

Mrs Oakland

Many of the teachers we have included so far have made a profound impact on young lives in the classroom. It was their interactions with particular kids during lessons that made such a lasting impression, but Sally Oakland is a little different. Whilst her music lessons were legendary in the secondary school where she taught – each one a festival of energy and creativity – it was all the other things she did which really enabled her to make her mark with generations of students. Her music department was a whole world of its own, a wonderfully chaotic spider's web of leads and extensions, feeding what seemed like an entire orchestra of musical instruments, both electronic and traditional. As soon as an intrepid young enquirer stepped over the threshold, they could not help but be caught up in a magic kingdom of rhythms and melodies and harmonies.

From the moment she arrived in the morning to the moment she left at the end of the day, at whatever time that was, Sally was immersed in the business of making music. An accomplished performer herself, she fizzed and buzzed with her passion for the subject. She was in school long before most of her colleagues on Tuesdays to run a practice session for the school orchestra. She would remain in her empire every break and lunchtime, running sessions for those experimenting with and learning different instruments. It goes without saying that she stayed on after school to run more clubs, more choirs, and more opportunities for all the different bands and groups who wanted to create music.

For a young Bethany Oaten, this was what so appealed to her about Sally: the way she went the extra mile out of lesson time to provide not just opportunities for music but also a safe haven for those who sought it, away from the hurly-burly of school life and yet integral to it. Bethany had started to learn to play the flute before she arrived at secondary school, so she knew that she would gravitate towards the music department. What she had not anticipated was how that music area would become her second home. For many kids at the school, break or dinner time was a chance to head to the dinner hall before hanging out in the fairly cramped school playground with not much to do. Bethany, and all those for whom music was their focus of attention, headed straight for Sally's room. They were made to feel welcome to munch a quick sandwich there (rather to the consternation of the school premises staff who would have to clean up when everyone had gone home!). Other teachers would use breaktimes to head for the staffroom, passing by the kettle as they went. Sally didn't seem to be confined by such needs: she was working with kids making music all through the day. An inspiration!

However, Sally was more than just a wonderful music teacher. She made all those students – like Bethany – feel as though the music department was their second family. She made it clear that she was always there for any of them if they needed a listening ear, and she meant it. There was one occasion when things were not working out as Bethany had hoped, and she headed for Sally. Sally listened to her and made her feel important in a totally non-judgemental way. She made her a cup of tea and Bethany just knew that she could unburden herself. Crucially she felt that she could trust Sally. Once Bethany had taken a moment to get herself back on an even keel, Sally took it upon herself to go and find the teacher whose lesson Bethany was supposed to be in to let her know what was going on. All of this in her non-contact time, which to most teachers is sacrosanct! Not to Sally. She would always go the extra mile.

Bethany credits Sally with going further than that. There is a lot of talk about young people's mental health at present, and it would be a churlish colleague who didn't think it was important. Doing something meaningful about it, however, is a different matter. Sally knew that Bethany was a very talented and hard-working student across the board, but she went out of her way to make sure that Bethany was looking after herself properly, balancing her appetite for academic success with the need for relaxation time to recharge her batteries and the need to keep things in perspective. Bethany says that she always felt comfortable in the music room, and playing her flute became a natural thing to do when she felt stressed. She says that it is still her main form of stress relief. Bethany has gone on to study medicine, but music is still embedded into her weekly routine. She has had some life-changing opportunities to play her flute in places as far afield (geographically and/or aspirationally) as the Italian lakes and the Royal Albert Hall, which would have been beyond her wildest dreams as a young child.

As teachers, we never know what impact we have on our pupils. Bethany remembers the difficulties she was having in her first year at the school with playing a particular piece for a short show she was in about the Egyptians. She was really worried that she was going to mess it up, but Sally took her to one side and went through it with her slowly until she had got it. Sally never gave up on her, even when she was wobbling. Going from strength to strength from that moment on, Bethany played the flute in every subsequent school show. On one of the end-of-year trips to Alton Towers, Sally joined a group of students, all of whom had been heavily involved in the music department, on the Congo River Rapids. Inevitably of course they all got soaked. Bethany bought the obligatory photograph and still has it in a keyring which she keeps on her desk all these years later. That's some impact!

Bethany still keeps in touch with Sally and actually returned to the school to play in the band during the summer show. She sat next to Sally, who was playing the violin. Bethany regards it as one of the greatest privileges of her life to play alongside someone who was such an inspiration to her. She would like to say a huge thank you to Sally for helping her to become the person she is today by supporting her academically and pastorally throughout her time at the school. She knows that she wouldn't be where she is today without Sally Oakland.

Bethany during early high school days

Bethany, present day

Sally, still performing

The difference?

Chris is a modest sort of fellow and in his time taught somewhere in the region of 30,000 lessons. Now, being the sort of chap that he is, he wouldn't lay claim to them all being absolute classics, but he would be disappointed if the overall tally of pretty decent lessons wasn't a healthy one. It is a source of never-ending wonderment to him that whenever he meets up with former students and they reminisce about the old times, when asked what they remember in particular, they wax lyrical about the trips to Paris which he organised, they bristle with pride at the mere mention of the school productions which he led or the nail-biting finishes to cricket matches for which he trained them. Not a mention of one of those fabrications of fantasy formed out of the elixir of excellence which were his lessons! Not one!

For many, many young people it is those extracurricular experiences of trips, clubs, shows or sporting fixtures which stay in the mind long after the poetry of their lessons has evaporated into the mists of memory. We had an interesting experience doing some training for a school in France. One of the differences we found between what happens here and what happens there was that there was much more of a focus there on just the academic diet, to the exclusion – we felt – of all the extracurricular activities which oil the wheels of schools in the UK system. Kids see a different side of you once you are outside the classroom. You are no longer just a purveyor of maths or geography; you become a real person, so our message is to get involved as much as you possibly can in every sinew of the life of your school. Time spent running the chess club, helping with costumes for the school show or coaching the netball team is never wasted. Kids need a reason to want to come to school and it is these extras which help to provide that reason. Furthermore, it will help you to build positive relationships, especially with some of the more reluctant learners. For Sally, music was her world but for others it will be hobbies or sport or drama. It doesn't matter what the activity is, getting involved will pay big dividends.

CAN YOU ADD ENRICHMENT BEYOND THE CLASSROOM?

The second thing which stands out from Bethany's testimony is the way in which she talks about how Sally handled the situation when she was having a tough time and turned to her for help. She specifically draws attention to the way Sally listened to her in a non-judgemental way. We live in a society in which instant judgements are made on a daily – and, indeed, hour-by-hour – basis, fed by the power of social media. We feel pressurised into making judgements instantly: do we agree with this or that? Which side are we on? Who is right and who is wrong? Feelings are not like that. We all have feelings and feelings are neither right nor wrong. Bethany was feeling overwhelmed, yet finding it hard to admit this to herself or anyone else. She was fearful of saying that she wasn't coping, but what Sally did was to listen and then nurture her. We all need love, care, nurturing, nutrition and warmth to survive and thrive. Sally gave Bethany her time and wrapped her in all the goodness and kindness she could muster to help her to feel good again.

In Bethany's case, she was struggling and found it hard to admit that she was less than perfect. Sally did not judge. She listened and made her a cup of tea. In a similar way we have encountered many young people who make mistakes in school. They may behave in an inappropriate way – at which point the traditional response tends to be to go down the route of an agreed system of penalties, accompanied by a good telling-off. This is how the stereotypical teacher will always behave in kids' minds. That shouty, naggy, bossy person personified by the Bash Street Kids' teacher in the *Beano*, who shouts at you and tells you off for being wrong. It is our experience, especially with some of the more reluctant learners, that some kids have a long backstory of messing up and then being told off. It is just how it is. It is our contention that no amount of punishment or penalty will turn them around. As long as they feel that they are being judged to be 'bad', and having that label stuck on them, they will behave accordingly. The most effective way to start to turn things around is to listen in a totally non-judgemental way. Separate the behaviour from the child. Start from the premise that the child is a good person, albeit one who has not made the best choices in terms of behaviour, and make sure they know that this is how you see them. Often, they are so conditioned by years of being told off that their emotional antennae will not pick up what you are saying. Make sure that they know that you are listening to them in a non-judgemental way. It could work wonders for you.

MENTAL HEALTH MATTERS

The last thing about Sally which we note from Bethany's story is how she explicitly took on responsibility for Bethany's mental health. Britain is the nation of the stiff upper lip and we are uneasy talking about our mental and emotional health. Indeed, this has been institutionally under-recognised in our health system, which until quite recently has focused almost entirely on physical well-being, but that is changing and for the better. It is no longer taboo to talk about anxiety and depression, and it is no longer assumed that everyone is OK unless something goes catastrophically wrong. There are many high-profile people who are now talking openly about their own mental health battles, and this increasing awareness is leading to the understanding that we need to take a much more proactive role in tackling mental health, not just reacting when problems surface. Sally helped Bethany to understand the importance of finding a balance in life between work and play. Like many young people, Bethany was set upon doing as well as she possibly could at school and was putting massive amounts of pressure on herself. Sally helped her to reset the dial, and we know that this important life lesson still helps Bethany to find the time for activities which are wholesome and therapeutic in a world which exerts almost constant pressure.

> *Weather gods in schools take sunshine everywhere and build positive relationships.*[1]

1 Toward, Malton and Henley, *The Decisive Element*, p. 21.

Conclusion:

The top ten traits of *that* teacher

It has been an incredible journey writing this book. We have laughed out loud, been goggle-eyed with amazement and shed several tears as we read the nominations and wrote the stories. It has been a privilege to have been allowed into the lives of so many people to learn how their teachers changed their futures. We could have written a book twice this size as the stories kept coming. But we've chosen only 19 as, collectively, they really illustrated what *that* teacher 'looks' like.

When we started work on this book, we had no idea how the stories we were hoping to receive would materialise, what they would be about and, most importantly, what they would tell us about teachers who change lives. All teachers change lives. From the moment they interact with a pupil on their very first day on a placement as a trainee, they begin the process. Many changes will be small and a lot of them academic or creative as part of the learning they deliver in the classroom. A lot of these changes you can use to create data and measure improvement, and the government and Ofsted is particularly keen on doing so. But then there are other forms of change: the stuff you can't easily measure. The spiritual, moral, social and cultural learning that teachers deliver. The happiness and fun they create. The feeling of warmth they pass on. And the passion they infect their pupils with.

Sometimes the change a teacher creates is a supernova: a change of such proportion that it totally changes the life of an individual. All the teachers who we have written about in this book have done just that. To the people who nominated them, they are super teachers. So, in case you are wondering, and we hope you are, if you could distil the key features of *that* teacher, what would their different traits be?

Now, we are not suggesting that you should read this next section and model yourself based on exactly what we say. Far from it. If you've learned anything from the stories in the book, you will have noticed that each one has a different context and that there are different personalities at play. Sorry to be party poopers but there is no one-size-fits-all super teacher. But what is quite clear is that there are some things we can learn from these teachers, so that every teacher could develop their own teaching persona within their context to help them be the very best teacher they can be.

But be warned, it's a long road. Our view is that being a teacher is a learning journey as much as being a pupil is. In Gary's last year of headship he carried out an observation of an NQT's lesson. It was a fantastic lesson and the teacher had the kids just where she wanted them. But there was one thing she did that Gary had never seen before. It was nothing complicated, just a different way of asking the pupils for contributions. Gary, who was still teaching a GCSE English class, used the idea in his next lesson. You are never too long in the tooth to learn.

So, here are the top ten traits (in no particular order) that the very best of our profession exhibit. You'll notice that data and progress measures don't feature. This is because, if you have got these things in your armoury, your kids are going to be bouncing along in their learning.

1. Positive relationships

In every classroom someone will be in charge. It will either be the kids (or the loudest and most unruly subgroups within the class) or it will be the teacher. It was ever thus!

In the days of yore, teachers relied on an assumption of natural authority. Children were expected to do as they were told and if they didn't, they faced punishment, usually physical punishment. The teacher who relies on the cane has thankfully long gone, as the world has changed. All the teachers we have featured have been nominated because of the culture they have created within their classroom – a culture based on a relentless drive to build positive relationships with the kids, a culture that is one of their hallmarks.

This is no easy fix with kids whose first instinct is often to see what they can get away with. We have met many teachers, too many, whose instinctive recourse is to the penalties prescribed by the school's behaviour policy. The teachers we love to remember are the ones who rarely have to resort to this. They incrementally build, over time, great relationships with each and every child, making them feel valued and appreciated. They listen and make sure that the pupil they are talking to knows they are listening. They make sure that the child knows that they know them, rate them and see them as a good person, even on the days when it all goes wrong. Psychologists refer to applying 'strokes', dispensing that feel-good factor which will make a child feel good about themselves and about their potential as a learner.[1] It is the metaphorical equivalent of a helping of school dinner custard: warm, nutritious and nourishing. This is 'relational value'. In every relationship we yearn to feel valued – and the very best teachers create the relationships that ensure this happens.

Positive relationships underpin everything you do as a teacher, and once created – remember, it's the responsibility of the teacher to do this as they don't just happen by accident – teaching is so much easier.

2. Praise and positivity[2]

During the process of writing this book we spoke many times, both on our phones and via the magic of video call. Gary's border collie, Sam, loves it. He recognises Chris's voice immediately and rushes over to see how he has managed to get inside that little box! Chris talks to him and tells him he's a good boy and Sam excitedly wags his tail in his best 'pleased as Punch' manner. After all, he is a good boy and who doesn't like a bit of praise?

It seems to be in our nature to desire praise, to get that feel-good hit when someone tells us we have done well. Just do an internet search and you'll find many articles on why we crave praise and other forms of approval and positive feedback. So why not make the most of this as a teacher? Praise is a major tool in developing positive relationships, resilience and challenge in the classroom. It can be used to great effect as a motivator, turning a pupil from a miscreant who does the bare minimum to a star performer who works hard every lesson.

Praise, however, can go badly wrong, so be warned. We strongly recommend that you praise your pupils for effort and link that to the positive outcome you have spotted. Make sure your classes understand

1 Ian Stewart and Vann Joines, *TA Today: A New Introduction to Transactional Analysis* (Nottingham and Chapel Hill, NC: Lifespace Publishing, 1987), p. 77.

2 For much more detail on this, see Toward, Henley and Malton, *The Decisive Element*.

that you praise for effort – and that the rewards you give are for effort – and eventually you will establish a can-do ethos in your classroom. The kids will give it a go and not be afraid to fail.

Alongside this, the very best teachers have an unwavering positive approach. They project happiness, fun and enthusiasm, providing the role model that so many kids need. They infect their classes with positive energy, even on a gloomy Friday afternoon just after a wet lunchtime. It is in classrooms like theirs that great learning takes place and the kids leave looking forward to their next visit.

3. Great lessons

This seems to be a bit of a 'state the obvious' trait. And we are sure that there has never been a teacher who set out to teach a mediocre lesson. But even the most biddable, can-do, positive class of kids will flounder if the lesson doesn't tick certain boxes. These, then, are our top tips for great lessons:

- Be demonstrably excited to be teaching the topic, even if it's not your favourite area.
- Assume the kids have zero interest in the topic, so your task is to generate that interest.
- Consider the 'what's in it for me?' factor. How are you going to get buy-in from the kids?
- Know your class. Know the individuals in the class. Learn what they are interested in. We call this 'kid culture' and there's more to follow about it. Build kid culture into your lessons. You can differentiate for different target groups – some, for example, might be into a particular sport, another group a certain band, and so on.
- Create or find brilliant resources to help develop wow moments and awe and wonder, or to help embed learning, especially with visual and kinaesthetic learners.

- Build in opportunities for different learning styles with room for those who are visual learners, interpersonal and intrapersonal learners and kinaesthetic ones. Give opportunities for the talkers to talk and the ones who like to work it out themselves to do so.[3]

- Model. Strut your funky stuff on your own catwalk.[4] Show the kids and talk them through the thinking behind the concepts you are teaching. Illustrate how to do it and elevate this by describing your thinking.

- Engage and challenge them. If you've established a can-do ethos, then they will understand that you have high expectations. In your classroom, you'll be teaching kids with a range of abilities. Challenge them all, ensuring that they all have the right amount of scaffolding and support to get there.

- Pop in mini plenaries, to recall material, check on progress and deal with misconceptions.

- Never be afraid to change tack mid lesson, no matter how much planning you have put in. If you see a path open up towards a different approach that you think will be better, take it.

- Take risks and have fun with your pupils.

4. Feedback

The current vogue on television is for a plethora of programmes in which contestants try their hand at something and then are marked by the experts. Whether it is *Strictly Come Dancing* or the *Bake Off* or *Sewing Bee* of the Great British variety, the format is the same. For those intent on progressing in the competition, feedback is crucial for their prospects of improving their performance. We noted a recurrent theme in the stories given to us of teachers who encouraged and nurtured the talent of the person nominating them by giving great feedback.

3 See Chapter 10, on Mr Buraselis, for more detail on our views on learning styles.

4 We never thought we'd reference a Right Said Fred song in one of our books!

It has become a little bit of a theme of ours when we work in schools to convince the staff to rename their marking policy a 'feedback policy'. Marking, after all, is only one part of feedback and is not appropriate in several school settings. Feedback works best when it is immediate. Kids don't have enormously long memory spans (and nor do we!), so feedback next lesson in the form of carefully crafted, formulaic written responses in an exercise book or folder is less likely to have an impact than instant feedback on the day – and, of course, this can be oral or written. If you ask any teacher to name the principal sources of workload stress, marking is never far from the top of the list. Hours spent scribing comments during evenings and weekends are wasted if they don't result in more learning. Giving meaningful and spontaneous feedback is a skill which the most successful teachers develop. It is good for workload and good for the kids.

5. Mr or Mrs Different[5]

It is a never-ending source of fascination to us that at any social gathering, if you throw out the question, 'Who was your best teacher at school?' you are guaranteed a conversation. We even do it during our training sessions. Of course, you do sometimes find that – like unfortunate fishermen – your net comes up empty. There are some folk out there who genuinely don't have anyone who immediately springs to mind, but many people come up with at least one teacher, and that in itself poses a question. Each of us will have had 30, 40, maybe even 50 different teachers during our passage through the different stages of our education, but there are usually only one or two who hit the bullseye. These are the ones who leave an indelible impression in our minds because they were different to all the rest.

The reason why they were different varies massively. In one of our workshops, we often play a clip of an American flight attendant called David – instead of doing the safety announcement at the beginning of every flight in the usual uninspiring fashion, he does it as a rap.[6] The result is that he transforms the whole cabin and energises his audience, who, incidentally, are therefore much more likely to heed his message – most of us, frankly, let it go in one ear and out the other.

5 Other titles, appellations, honorifics, etc. are available.
6 See https://www.youtube.com/watch?v=G9lZV_828OA.

David was different and, similarly, all of the teachers in this book are different in their own way. Some, like Jason Wood, are extroverts. Others, like Mrs Brandow, were cast in a quieter mould but had a huge impact where others had not made much impression. Yet more, like Mr Tweedy, got through where others had failed. The crucial thing is that they were all Mr or Mrs Different.

We'd recommend you ask yourself the question: what makes you different from the rest of the teachers in your school? What is your unique selling point (USP)?

6. Outside the classroom

We were always surprised by colleagues who told us they didn't like bumping into their pupils when out and about at the weekend. We've always seen it as an honour if a pupil, an ex-pupil or a parent recognises us. It's happened to us both in the most unusual of places, from a castle in the Scottish Highlands to a Swiss lakeside. Typically, if the recognition goes further than a smile and a wave, there will be some form of conversation – especially if it is with an ex-pupil – about past times. Rarely, however, do they want to chat about the day-to-day shenanigans in our classrooms, but tend to instantly bring up fond memories of the experiences they had with us on trips or whilst involved in clubs and shows. And we know this doesn't just apply to us, as hundreds of colleagues and delegates at our presentations have told us the same.

There is something about gathering kids together outside of the normal sphere of working that adds an extra fruity layer of educational gateau. It may be the fact that you communicate with the kids differently. It's possible that they see you in a different light and not just as their English teacher or head of year. It could be that the experience you are giving them is just so different to their norm. Or it might just be that they are grateful to you for giving up your free time to give them a new experience. One of the added bonuses these extras brings is that your relationship with the participants changes. You become more than their teacher. You develop a bond that cannot be broken as you have a shared experience that is not a straightforward teacher–pupil one.

We know you are busy and, crumbs, it's a tough job at the best of times, so you'd be forgiven if you raised your eyebrows at the mere recommendation that you do something with your pupils outside your classroom. But we are indeed going to suggest that, because we know that not only will it take you to another level of being *that* teacher, but it will also bring you some of the best memories of your teaching career.

Yes, it works both ways. There is hardly a week that goes by when we do not reminisce about one of those many added extras we've either put on ourselves or been involved in. They, in many respects, have been the best things we have done in our careers and are different ways of changing lives.

7. Above and beyond

We have met so many astonishing colleagues over the years who have given every sinew of their strength to help kids in their own individual ways. Some would happily accept that they were honest journeymen and women who gave their best in and around school, but there are some who stand out because they went way beyond what would normally be expected. There were those who ran extracurricular sports teams, performing arts activities or school trips, and then there were others who would give of their time to individual kids when the need arose. These are teachers who stand out: they dress up, they take part in most events, they find ways to help kids in different ways, they do things they don't have to do.

The teacher who takes the time to thank parents who have taken the trouble to come to parents' evening, the teacher who gives a parent a quick call to say how well their child has done in a particular lesson, the teacher who gives up precious non-contact time to spend with a child who has come unstuck, the teacher who keeps in touch when a child has to have time off school, the teacher who spots potential in a child that the child has never seen in themself – all of these colleagues make a difference and, by going above and beyond, they make a lasting impression on that child.

8. Inclusivity

Schools can be pretty brutal places if you are a little bit different for any reason. Bullying is never far away, in whatever form it presents itself, and the pressure on kids who don't quite fit the image required by the peer police can be relentless. For many kids, the teacher who rescued them from feeling that they didn't belong or that they didn't fit for whatever reason is guaranteed a place in their hearts for the rest of time. Again, we stress that 'teacher' here extends to all the staff in the school: all adults are role models and educators. A premises officer, just as much as a teaching assistant (TA) or a school librarian, could be the one whose antennae twitch when they sense that all is not well. They could become the first person to make that child feel that they matter.

In the classroom, there is always a special place in the pantheon of greatness for those teachers who open up the doors of learning for a child in a subject area where they previously lacked any aptitude or interest. We are hard-wired to be our own harshest critics. We berate ourselves for being hopeless at public speaking or no good at DIY. The super special teachers are the ones who make kids believe that there is something in that subject or area of learning for them, that they shouldn't write it off. The skill of wonderful teachers, like Mr Harvey, is that they make the learning inclusive and accessible to every child.

9. Pastoral responsibilities

We'd love to tell the maths teachers out there that their subject is the most important in the curriculum. That would make them smile. However, we can't. Nor can we say that for any of the exam subjects on the curriculum. Sorry. Whilst your subjects are super important, we strongly believe that every one of them is underpinned by the quality of the pastoral side of the school.

How kids feel, how they are emotionally and spiritually, how they feel about coming to school, how they feel about going home, whether they feel safe, understood, cared for, supported, wanted, listened to ... we could go on ... has a direct impact on the academic side of the school. Lessons, quite simply, cannot be as good if pastoral care is not done well.

When both of us started out in our careers, we were introduced to the world of pastoral care. This was entirely new to us! We'd spent years learning how to teach our subject and the idea that we would have to add another 'subject' to our repertoire was a sudden and steep learning curve. Luckily, both of us had brilliant mentors and soon discovered the huge rewards of being form tutors. The honour of being the teacher who gathers a single group of pupils every day, not to teach them French or design – in our cases – but to provide support for them as they grow through the school, has always been a highlight of each of our teaching careers.[7] In primary and infant schools, there is even more opportunity for such pastoral care as class teachers have so much contact time with their pupils across the school day.

But it's not all about what you do in those sessions designated as 'tutor time' or 'class time' or 'pastoral time'. Every lesson, whatever the subject, needs pastoral care seamlessly slotted in amongst the subject stuff that's going on. Just occasionally we have met teachers who think that pastoral issues are someone else's problem and pass the buck to a head of key stage or year, but you won't find anyone like that in this book. Brilliant teachers and superb school leaders across the world understand this and make sure they deliver high-quality care for their pupils.

10. Kid culture

Whilst there is a music artist called Kid Culture, he's not what we're referring to here. (And props if you were familiar with him already – we stumbled across him online when googling the term.) What we are talking about is being 'down with the kids'!

What are the kids in your classes interested in? How much do you know about their likes and the things that make them sit up and listen? How many are into dance? Who likes rap music, who likes garage? Which ones are avid watchers of *Strictly Come Dancing*? Who, along with her sister, breeds budgies? Which computer games are they into, do they like particular sports, watch certain movies, collect key fobs, cycle, ice skate, and so on? We challenge you to go down your class list and write down the interests of every child next to their name. If

7 Gary is still in contact with many young people – now not so young – from his first tutor group and feels wonderfully honoured by that.

there are blanks, particularly next to a pupil you're having trouble engaging, do some homework.

We advise trainees and NQTs to do a simple exercise with their classes. A confidential survey between them and you called, 'Things you would like to tell me'. This can include any manner of questions and can add to your knowledge of them as part of your pastoral care responsibilities, but additionally, simply asking what their interests are gives you another opportunity to differentiate learning for engagement. This can be as simple as providing worksheets with graphics on. Kids who are into football can write their answers in the white hexagons on a picture of a football. Those who are into dance write in silhouettes of dancers. Get the idea? But you can take this much further. Chris once differentiated a lesson about *Romeo and Juliet* to engage one coasting student who he had learned was into the girl band Girls Aloud. He designed a whole lesson using the band as characters in the play. His student was hooked. She worked super hard and bounced back into class the next lesson with a smile. Typically, you have to work a bit more than this, but for this student, who arrived at the lesson to hear her favourite band playing, that one focused effort was enough. She raised her game long term.

It can take a bit of work to keep on top of this, but it's worth it. Keep tabs on the changing tides of interests in your classroom. Keep an eye on what is happening in the world that might be a winner for you. Is there a particular TV show or a new superhero movie coming out, or a major sporting event around the corner? We had the privilege of watching an amazing Year 7 lesson in which the science teacher had worked out that a large number of his class loved *Doctor Who*. They entered a darkened lab after break. He was waiting at the door, greeting them in costume as the Doctor. His TA was in character as his assistant, twirling a sonic screwdriver. The TARDIS was rotating around the interactive whiteboard with the show's theme tune playing in the background. As the class settled, the display magically changed to a Dalek, screeching 'Exterminate!' At the flick of a switch by the TA, a shelf of bottles containing coloured liquids was backlit. The kids were mesmerised. 'The Earth is being invaded by Daleks,' the fake Doctor said, 'and you have 45 minutes to save it. One of those bottles contains a liquid that will kill the Daleks.' The lesson was on acids and alkalis, and the kids – even those who were not into *Doctor Who* but nonetheless were incredibly caught up in the enthusiasm of the rest – worked as if they were really saving the world!

Kid culture: it can be magic.

Epilogue

Top authors and playwrights use epilogues, so we thought we'd better have one.

We began this book by telling you a little about our stories and about how we joined the amazing profession of teaching. We were fizzing and buzzing about the job then and nothing has changed now that we don't go to school every day. We love passing on our experience to the new incredible generations of teachers we see in our presentations and to those who have read our books. We cannot see a time when we will lose our love of teaching.

We hope that you have enjoyed this book and, more importantly, spotted how teachers make never-ending changes that ripple through time. Changing one life changes many more.

If you're thinking about becoming a teacher, we hope we have given you a picture of what you can achieve if you do join the wonderful world of the classroom. If you are already in the profession, your inputs have already begun to reverberate their way to the 22nd century. You're changing the lives of the kids you teach right now, and your brilliance will rub off on their offspring and all the others they will encounter in their life. From there, it's only a small bounce to the grandchildren of your class. Hundreds of people will benefit from the fact that you made a difference for one pupil. Imagine how many that will add up to by the time you've taught for 10, 20 or 30 years!

The great use of life is to spend it for something that outlasts it.

William James[1]

1 See https://quoteinvestigator.com/2012/11/28/great-life/.

Bibliography

Anonymous (2020). A letter to … the teacher who inspired my young son, *The Guardian* (11 April 2020). Available at: https://www.theguardian.com/lifeandstyle/2020/apr/11/a-letter-to-the-teacher-who-inspired-my-youngson?CMP=Share_iOSApp_Other.

Attenborough, David (1984). *The Living Planet* (London: William Collins).

Bennett, Rosemary (2014). We've never had it so good: 1957 was the happiest year, *The Times* (24 January). Available at: https://www.thetimes.co.uk/article/weve-never-had-it-so-good-1957-was-the-happiest-year-ctx8whpgw.

Bradbury, Ray (1953). *The Golden Apples of the Sun* (New York: Doubleday and Company).

Briggs, Saga (2013). The Matthew effect: what is it and how can you avoid it in your classroom?, *InformED* (1 July). Available at: https://www.opencolleges.edu.au/informed/features/the-matthew-effect-what-is-it-and-how-can-you-avoid-it-in-your-classroom/.

Bryson, Bill (2019). *The Body: A Guide for Occupants* (London: Transworld).

Butter, Nick (2020). *Running the World: My World Record Adventure to Run a Marathon in Every Country on Earth* (London: Transworld).

Churchill Centre and Churchill Museum (2009). *Finest Hour: The Journal of Winston Churchill*, 143 (Summer). Available at: https://winstonchurchill.org/wp-content/uploads/2017/03/Finest_Hour_143.pdf.

Cope, Andy, Gary Toward and Chris Henley (2015). *The Art of Being a Brilliant Teacher* (Carmarthen: Crown House Publishing).

Fell, Jason (2012). Guy Kawasaki: no 'secret sauce' for tech success, *Entrepreneur* (1 June). Available at: https://www.entrepreneur.com/article/223691.

Ginott, Haim (1972). *Teacher and Child: A Book for Parents and Teachers* (New York: Macmillan).

Godfrey-Smith, Peter (2018). *Other Minds: The Octopus and the Evolution of Intelligent Life* (London: William Collins).

Harrigan, Joe (2020). Leona Harris: Rossendale-born nurse to feature on ITV advent calender and new Dan Walker book, *Lancashire Telegraph* (20 November). Available at: https://www.lancashiretelegraph.co.uk/news/18885536.leona-harris-rossendale-born-nurse-feature-itv-advent-calender-new-dan-walker-book/.

Hemingway, Ernest (2004 [1950]). *Across the River and into the Trees* (London: Arrow Books).

Henriques, Gregg (2016). Relational value: a core human need, *Psychology Today* (23 June). Available at: https://www.psychologytoday.com/blog/theory-knowledge/201206/relational-value.

Milligan, Spike (2014 [1963]). *Puckoon* (London: Penguin).

Mohdin, Aamna (2019). Nish Kumar gets frosty reception at Lord's Taverners charity feast, *The Guardian* (3 December). Available at: https://www.theguardian.com/uk-news/2019/dec/03/nish-kumar-gets-frosty-reception-at-lords-taverners-charity-feast.

Nuwer, Rachel (2014). Andy Warhol probably never said his celebrated 'fifteen minutes of fame' line, *Smithsonian Magazine* (8 April). Available at: https://www.smithsonianmag.com/smart-news/andy-warhol-probably-never-said-his-celebrated-fame-line-180950456/.

Schools Week (2017). When did schools ban corporal punishment? (25 January). Available at: https://schoolsweek.co.uk/when-did-schools-ban-corporal-punishment/.

Selby, Jenn (2020). Teacher walks hundreds of miles to hand-deliver 7,500 school meals to his hungry students, *iNews* (18 July). Available at: https://inews.co.uk/news/teacher-walks-deliver-free-school-meals-grimsby-556960.

Stewart, Ian and Vann Joines (1987). *TA Today: A New Introduction to Transactional Analysis* (Nottingham and Chapel Hill, NC: Lifespace Publishing).

Strauss, Valerie (2020). John Lennon's report card at 15: 'He has too many of the wrong ambitions', *The Washington Post* (9 October). Available at: https://www.washingtonpost.com/education/2020/10/09/john-lennons-report-card-15-he-has-too-many-wrong-ambitions/.

Toward, Gary, Mick Malton and Chris Henley (2018). *The Decisive Element: Unleashing Praise and Positivity in Schools* (Carmarthen: Crown House Publishing).

Wright, Ian (2016). *A Life in Football: My Autobiography* (London: Constable).

About the authors

In 2015 Gary and Chris decided that, for the first time since they had each been 5 years old, they wouldn't go to school every day any more, having chalked up a combined 70 years of experience in the classroom, much of it in positions of leadership. However, the passion for education and for schools continued to burn bright and they set out on a journey to pass on the torch and inspire new generations of classroom practitioners, working together as a dynamic duo known collectively as Decisive Element. They have travelled all over the UK training teachers and speaking at conferences – and they have also delivered sessions in Europe, presenting in French.

They have also co-authored, along with Andy Cope, *The Art of Being a Brilliant Teacher* – which is now selling across the world and has recently been translated into Simplified Chinese. They have since added *The Art of Being a Brilliant NQT*, *The Art of Being a Brilliant Middle Leader* and *The Art of Being a Brilliant Classroom Assistant* to their portfolio, and worked with Mick Malton to write *The Decisive Element: Unleashing Praise and Positivity in Schools*.

Gary has written two novels, *One 4 for Sorrow* and *The Magpie*, and – unable to resist the lure of being back in the classroom – he often goes into secondary schools and delivers an exciting free presentation based on *The Magpie*, which is a historically accurate novel set in the trenches of the First World War. Chris is a funeral celebrant and a qualified cricket umpire.

Gary and Chris deliver presentations and keynotes based on their books to audiences across the UK and Europe.

gary@decisiveelement.co.uk chris@decisive-element.co.uk

www.decisive-element.co.uk @PositiveWeather

The Art of Being a Brilliant Classroom Assistant

Gary Toward, Chris Henley and Andy Cope

ISBN 978-178583022-8

Based on the authors' combined 70 plus years of experience, *The Art of Being a Brilliant Classroom Assistant* by Andy Cope, Chris Henley and Gary Toward is packed full of creative tips, techniques and strategies for anyone with the crucial role of supporting kids' learning.

There are many different names and acronyms for these amazing classroom practitioners: teaching assistants (TAs), learning support assistants (LSAs), cover supervisors, supply teachers, student mentors, higher level teaching assistants (HLTAs), learning partners – the list goes on. The title doesn't matter but the quality of support, interaction and learning does. Whether you work one-to-one with individual children, support small groups or work with a whole class – and whether you work in a primary, secondary or special setting – this book is packed with ideas to enhance your practice so you can best support children's learning, while looking out for your own well-being and enjoying your role.

The Art of Being a Brilliant Middle Leader

Gary Toward, Chris Henley and Andy Cope

ISBN 978-178583023-5

Gary, Chris and Andy cover the myriad of issues facing middle leaders with their customary mix of good humour and solid, experience-informed advice.

Topics covered include: starting a new role; whether in a new school or following internal promotion, what your colleagues and the kids will expect of you, identifying personal strengths and areas for further development, shifting your focus from your to-do list to your to-be list, having an impact, building rapport and a team ethos, planting seeds of positivity across the school, tips for holding effective meetings, how to plan improvement which works for your team and meets the expectations of senior leaders, planning, implementing and evaluating change, dealing with negative colleagues, overcoming issues and personnel problems, understanding and owning your thinking, celebrating successes, modelling and sharing best practice and developing a brilliant team.

The Art of Being a Brilliant NQT

Gary Toward and Chris Henley Edited by Andy Cope

ISBN 978-184590940-6

Everything an NQT always wanted to know about starting their teaching career but never dared to ask!

This book will take the NQT through a journey which starts with interviews, leads them through the first visit before taking up the job and then into the first hectic weeks and months. Light in touch but rich in content, it can be read around the pool during the holidays before the start of term or kept by the bedside or in a desk drawer for an emergency flick through once teaching gets under way! It expands on the stuff that teacher training touches on, but importantly provides a refreshing look at the nitty-gritty stuff that most training doesn't!

Topics explored include:

- getting a job
- dealing with workload
- discipline
- preparing lessons
- dealing with parents
- pastoral care
- being a form tutor
- dealing with colleagues
- marking
- assemblies
- career development and much more …

The Art of Being a Brilliant Teacher

Gary Toward, Chris Henley and Andy Cope

ISBN 978-184590941-3

Teaching is an art; with the right techniques, guidance, skills and practice, teachers can masterfully face any situation the classroom could throw at them. With their fresh perspectives, sage advice and a hint of silliness, Gary, Chris and Andy show teachers how to unleash their brilliance.

For any teacher who has ever had a class that are angels for colleagues but Lucifer incarnate as soon as they cross the threshold of their classroom. Or who realised too late that their best-laid lesson plans were doomed from the start. Or who had their energy and enthusiasm sapped by a mood-hoovering staffroom Grinch. These problems will be a thing of the past once they've mastered the art of being a brilliant teacher. With plenty of practical advice and top tips, this book will show them how.

The Decisive Element

Unleashing Praise and Positivity in Schools

Gary Toward, Mick Malton and Chris Henley

ISBN 978-178583312-0

Forget data. Forget league tables. Forget the national curriculum. Teachers are the true weather gods in education. The default outlook in schools at present, however, seems to be 'gloom'. Our schools' staff are under relentless pressure, and their ever-increasing workloads can make it easy to forget about the humans they work with. So what can teachers do to bring back the sunny weather and make pupils' school lives more joyous?

Gary, Mick and Chris believe that the answer lies in harnessing the power of praise and positivity.

In *The Decisive Element* they offer an uplifting antidote to the anxiety by sharing praise focused techniques that will help teachers and school leaders create an ethos of enthusiasm: one that reduces stress, fuels ambition and builds confidence – for staff and pupils alike. Crammed full of sound research, fresh ideas and top tips, this manifesto for positive mindsets celebrates the value of meaningful, impactful praise and shines a light on the myriad ways positivity can be unleashed to spark pupils' motivation and natural curiosity for learning.